The Connected Community

The Connected Community

Discovering the Health, Wealth,
and Power of Neighborhoods

Cormac Russell

John McKnight

Berrett–Koehler Publishers, Inc.

Berrett-Koehler Publishers, Inc. Tel: (510) 817-2277
1333 Broadway, Suite 1000 Fax: (510) 817-2278
Oakland, CA 94612-1921 www.bkconnection.com

ORDERING INFORMATION

Quantity sales. Special discounts are available on quantity purchases by corporations, associations, and others. For details, contact the "Special Sales Department" at the Berrett-Koehler address above.

Individual sales. Berrett-Koehler publications are available through most bookstores. They can also be ordered directly from Berrett-Koehler: Tel: (800) 929-2929; Fax: (802) 864-7626; www.bkconnection.com.

Orders for college textbook / course adoption use. Please contact Berrett-Koehler: Tel: (800) 929-2929; Fax: (802) 864-7626.

Distributed to the U.S. trade and internationally by Penguin Random House Publisher Services.

Berrett-Koehler and the BK logo are registered trademarks of Berrett-Koehler Publishers, Inc.

Printed in the United States of America

Berrett-Koehler books are printed on long-lasting acid-free paper. When it is available, we choose paper that has been manufactured by environmentally responsible processes. These may include using trees grown in sustainable forests, incorporating recycled paper, minimizing chlorine in bleaching, or recycling the energy produced at the paper mill.

Library of Congress Cataloging-in-Publication Data

Names: Russell, Cormac, author. | McKnight, John, 1931– editor.
Title: The connected community : discovering the health, wealth, and power of neighborhoods / Cormac Russell, John McKnight.
Description: First Edition. | Oakland, CA : Berrett-Koehler Publishers, [2022] | Includes bibliographical references and index.
Identifiers: LCCN 2022012434 (print) | LCCN 2022012435 (ebook) | ISBN 9781523002528 (paperback) | ISBN 9781523002535 (pdf) | ISBN 9781523002542 (epub) | ISBN 9781523002559
Subjects: LCSH: Community development. | Neighborhoods. | Neighborliness. | Social change.
Classification: LCC HN49.C6 R845 2022 (print) | LCC HN49.C6 (ebook) | DDC 307.1/4—dc23
/eng/20220428
LC record available at https://lccn.loc.gov/2022012434
LC ebook record available at https://lccn.loc.gov/2022012435

First Edition

30 29 28 27 26 25 24 23 22   10 9 8 7 6 5 4 3 2 1

Cover design: Mayapriya Long
Book design and production: Leigh McLellan Design. *Copyeditor:* Alice Rowan.
Proofreader: Mary Hazlewood. *Indexer:* Ken DellaPenta.

This book is dedicated to regular folks who have committed themselves to enhancing the common good of their neighborhoods. Thank you for all you do.

Contents

Foreword *by Parker J. Palmer*　　　　　　　　　　　　ix

Preface　　　　　　　　　　　　　　　　　　　　　　xiii

Introduction
What Lies beyond Disconnection?　　　　　　　　　　　1

PART ONE: DISCOVER　　　　　　　　　　　　　　17

Discover at a Glance　　　　　　　　　　　　18

Chapter 1　Homecoming:
Rediscovering the Value of Community　　　21

Chapter 2　The Hazards of the Wrong Map:
From What's Wrong to What's Strong　　　　31

Chapter 3　The Neighborhood Treasure Hunt:
Basic Building Blocks　　　　　　　　　　41

Three Tools for Discovery　　　　　　　53

PART TWO: CONNECT   57

Connect at a Glance   58

Chapter 4   Beyond Leaders toward Connectors   61

Chapter 5   The Community Is Waiting to Contribute   73

Chapter 6   The Seven Functions of Connected Communities   85

Three Tools for Connection   101

PART THREE: MOBILIZE   105

Mobilize at a Glance   106

Chapter 7   Diary of a Neighborhood Made Visible and Vibrant
Part 1: Step by Step from Crisis to Connected   109

Chapter 8   Diary of a Neighborhood Made Visible and Vibrant
Part 2: Step by Step from Envisioning to Collective Action   119

Chapter 9   The Role of the Useful Outsider   135

Three Tools for Mobilization   145

Conclusion
The Connected Community—Not So Wild a Dream!   151

The Connected Community at a Glance   159

Discussion Guide   165

Notes and Sources   175

Resource Guide 1: The We Can Game   177

Resource Guide 2: Chapter 5 Tables   187

Acknowledgments   191

Index   193

About the Authors   oo

About Nurture Development, the Community
Renewal Centre, and the ABCD Institute   oo

Foreword

Parker J. Palmer

When someone asks where we live, we normally respond by naming a city and perhaps a state or county. If we know and trust that person, we might share our street address.

But if the question goes deeper—"No, really, *where* do you live? Tell me about the community you call home"—and we can't offer much more than GPS coordinates, is there a *there* there for us? If we don't have a story to tell about the people and the human and natural history to be found just beyond our front door, do we really *live* there?

Many of us are hard-pressed to provide color commentaries on our own neighborhoods, and for that we pay a price. Our disconnection from "people and place" diminishes our quality of life. It's one of the root causes of a range of personal and political pathologies in today's industrialized societies.

Isolation and the loneliness that comes with it lead to illnesses of the mind and body. In an interactive community, where people know enough about one another to notice and care, those maladies would arise less often and be treated sooner when they do. Disconnection also means there's no "We the People" to shape their collective fate or hold power accountable. Authoritarian rulers work hard to separate people from one another by fanning the flames of mutual suspicion that burn civic community to the ground, leaving them free to rule as they will.

If these are among the concerns that led you to pick up this book, you were well led. Cormac Russell and John McKnight are leading advocates and practitioners of Asset-Based Community Development (ABCD), a movement that's been challenging and changing the thinking of everyone who works in the field of community development since 1993, when McKnight and John Kretzmann published the groundbreaking *Building Communities from the Inside Out.*

The ABCD movement is a practical and proven response to the failure of external approaches to community issues: Give the "experts" a lot of money and they will solve problems that ordinary citizens can't solve. As more than a few "urban renewal" efforts show, that arrogant, materialistic top-down approach has led to millions of wasted dollars and more than a few tragic consequences.

Positive and persistent social transformation always involves local residents finding ways to pool and invest their gifts in a common cause. But if that's going to happen, we first need to develop the X-ray vision and imagination that will allow us to see the human gifts that are so often hidden in plain sight. That's where the ABCD approach begins. It then proceeds to strategy and on-the-ground action as people seek to connect with one another, humanize their communities, and democratize their nation.

For me, ABCD's credibility as a movement is enhanced by the fact that it excludes no one in its approach, as illustrated by its work with people with developmental disabilities. McKnight tells a moving story about his friend Pat Worth, who had been labeled "mentally retarded" in his youth and warehoused in an institution. Pat managed to shed that label and escape from that place and build a new life, as he said, "through chance and good fortune."

Eventually, Pat had the vision for People First, which has grown into an international self-advocacy organization for people with disabilities. In Pat's words, "We are not disabled. We are 'dis' but not disabled; we're disconnected. We don't need services, we need community."

The last three words in that powerful statement apply to all of us. But unlike Pat Worth, a lot of us think of ourselves as powerless to do anything about it. We feel trapped by powerful external forces that make disconnection our lot, from segregated neighborhoods to economic forces that deprive us of personal and communal time.

Nothing worthy can happen when we give away our birthright gift of human agency. When we gather with others to build a better life together, whatever agency we have at our command multiplies many times over and builds collective confidence in our capacity to restore our common life. That's where this book can take us, with its well-tested array of tools and strategies for reclaiming and exercising agency in the creation of connected neighborhoods and communities.

This act of recovery begins where all creativity begins: in active imagination. Imagine, for a moment, all that may be hidden in the space beyond your front door. As the authors suggest, that very likely includes the following:

> The skills, knowledge, passions, and experiences of neighbors whose names you don't recall or barely know. The informal clubs and groups that you are not a member of. The local institutions that contribute in small but important ways that you never hear about. The physical gems that lay hidden in the built and natural environment, yet to be discovered by you and many of your neighbors. The cultural treasures buried behind invitations you have never received.

As this book unfolds, it reveals how ordinary folks can make these invisible treasures visible and vibrant for people who live adjacent to one another and want to relate to one another. As example after example shows, once this social capital becomes visible, it can be invested in powerful ways to renew our health, security, care, local economy, ecology, and food sovereignty.

What makes for a thriving nation? That's an urgent question today, when the bodies politic of many nations around the world are clearly in ill-health. The great American poet Walt Whitman had an answer,[1] penned around the start of the American Civil War, when the country's body politic seemed close to taking its last breath:

> *STATES!*
> *Were you looking to be held together by the lawyers?*
> *By an agreement on a paper? Or by arms?*
>
> *Away!*
> *I arrive, bringing these, beyond all the forces of courts and arms,*
> *These! to hold you together as firmly as the earth itself is held together.*

By "These!" Whitman meant the relationships that are forged between neighbors. If we are to thrive as human beings, if democracy is to work as intended, it will depend on what Whitman called "countless linked hands" across our respective lands. This book shows us how to keep working for that democratic vision through connected communities.

Parker J. Palmer is the author of ten books, including *Healing the Heart of Democracy,* and founder of the Center for Courage & Renewal. He is a former community organizer.

Preface

History teaches us that all sustainable change happens at the grassroots level and then spreads out from there to create further ripples of change. Some of these ripples combine to create big waves; most trigger countless small and unexpected impacts that overlap and intersect in ways we'll never know the full importance of. This book is written in the wake of local ripples made by regular people in their communities using what they have to secure what they need. Their stories largely go untold, because they are modest, and do not feature heroes or Hollywood endings.

There are no stories about great leaders or crusaders in these pages. *The Connected Community* is about places, and about the combined efforts of the people who make them vibrant and are made vibrant by them. It is about neighbors taking responsibility for their local communities so that they and those they love can have a decent life, and so that future generations can expect to do the same.

These community stories have much to teach us about getting better at being human together. The late South African theologian Bishop Desmond Tutu popularized the term *Ubuntu,* which means "a person is a person through other people" or "I am because we are." Through this word he emphasized a route toward a decent life, or what in this book we refer to as the *Good Life,* which is about collective effort and cooperation, not individualism and competition. *Ubuntu* is the opposite of the sentiments expressed in the famous Frank Sinatra song "I Did It My Way," which romanticizes the American idol known as the "rugged individual" or what some call the "self-made person." Individualism is a superhighway to a sick, depressed, and dissatisfied life and a fragmented society. *Ubuntu,* by contrast, says we are not self-reliant, we are other reliant; that life is not about self-fulfillment and leaning into work and money. Instead, a satisfying life is largely about leaning into our relationships and investing in our communities; it is about interdependence, not independence.

This book aligns with the principles of *Ubuntu,* then goes on to show how we can discover and create *Ubuntu* in everyday life, by making visible, connected, and vibrant the invisible ingredients that surround us, using an approach called Asset-Based Community Development (ABCD). By tracing the footsteps of social explorers around the world who have happened upon the Keys to the Good Life, we have made plain a three-stage process for making the journey from disconnected neighborhood to Connected Community. We define these three stages as Discover, Connect, and Mobilize.

In learning from these local community-led change efforts from around the world, we see three simple but incredibly inventive strategies being used (all of which are thoroughly explored in this book):

1. People form connections with their neighbors beyond their workplace, family, and friendship groups, because they know that neighbor-to-neighbor connections matter much more than most people realize.

2. They start addressing problems and possibilities by building on what's strong and local, not on what's wrong and external.

3. They view their neighborhoods as primary sites for the Good Life to flourish; in other words, for them, satisfying and sustainable growth is not just about personal development or institutional reform, as commonly assumed, but about the Connected Community and the health, wealth, and power of neighborhoods.

This book offers a window into how to build momentum and widespread participation by starting close to where regular people live their lives. Starting close to people's doorsteps is essential to long-term innovation, sustainable community, and economic development. In *The Connected Community* we see clearly why neighborhoods are the ideal scale at which to address many of the social and economic issues alive in the world today.

So, if you are interested in exploring what happens when residents from neighborhoods around the world discover what they care about enough to act upon it, and how that care ripples outward, then you are going to love this book. The added bonus is that we don't just share a range of inspiring international stories; we also describe in detail the ABCD practices and principles that are instinctively and successfully being used by neighborhood associations to co-produce the Good Life where they live, and to hold outside institutions to account when necessary.

We believe that one of the strengths of this book is the absence of "cookie cutter" or one-size-fits-all solutions. Instead it sticks with real-world practices and insights drawn from neighborhoods that are making lives better together. We invite you to consider whether these approaches are relevant in your context, but more important, to invent responses that best fit your own neighborhood journey. This book is the ultimate sounding board for neighbors building their communities from the inside out, and for those working in neighborhood development who are interested in sustainable, community-driven change.

The Connected Community will exist only when each of us can say of our neighborhood, *Ubuntu:* "I am because we are."

What Lies beyond Disconnection?

At the root of many of the world's problems is our disconnection from one another and from our natural surroundings. The laundry list of the side effects is long and overwhelming, from severe levels of depression to planetary destruction. Increased polarization is another serious global concern. It does not stop with just political partisanship but is "poisoning everyday interactions and relationships."[1] This division is a stark account of modern life, and solutions are needed because the consequences of not acting are too serious. Increasingly, people are awakening to the sense that we can no longer stand on the sidelines as spectators consuming the negative side effects of consumer culture.

But what to do?

Answers vary, from protesting intensely so that we may convince our leaders to get their act together, to investing in science and technology so that we can innovate our way out of these global crises. There are many versions of the "protest versus progress" debate and no end of clever suggestions as to how to do each one better and quicker. And though we think both have their place, in the absence of widespread participation at the local level, neither of them convinces us.

Whether dubbed eco-warriors or captains of industry, neither camp will win its crusade alone. The third party, which all too often is forgotten in this equation, is "us" and our local communities.

In this book, we propose a completely different stage on which to take action toward an alternative future. That stage is our neighborhood. Our starting point is not Wall Street, it's our street.

Our true north is what we term the Connected Community, from which we have drawn the title for this book. We define Connected Communities as places where residents nurture neighborhood relationships that enable people to work together to create a Good Life. This definition contrasts with approaches and outlooks that prioritize relationships outside the neighborhood, that separate neighbors from one another and promote individual survival over community well-being. Such approaches result in disconnected communities.

Our journey, then, is from disconnected to Connected Communities. Although we recognize that the word *community* means many different things, here we are zeroing in on just one definition: a group of people residing in a shared place called a neighborhood. We are using *neighborhood* as a catchall term to speak about all manner of small, bounded geographic communities, including but not exclusive to estates, square mile, block, village, town, favela, or parish. We also acknowledge dispersed communities and people living "off country" and dislocated from their indigenous lands.

What Brought Us to See the Connected Community as the Foundation?

Although we are advocating for grassroots change, we are not promoting an either-or argument of people power versus institutional or political change. We need both. We worry, though, that if we're waiting for our leaders to get their act together before *we* act, little will change in our lifetime. Change is not about one or the other party solving social and economic problems and other issues of disconnection; it is about making change happen from the inside out, because for most neighborhoods around the world the cavalry are not coming to save the day, and if they *are* coming, it's to build a strip mall or shopping center.

Nearly thirty years ago, John McKnight, one of the authors of this book, coauthored a book called *Building Communities from the Inside Out: A Path Toward Finding and Mobilizing a Community's Assets.*[2] It became affectionately known as "The Green Book." Since its publication in 1993, more than 120,000 copies have been sold, and a further 20,000 have been gifted for free to communities around the world. The Green Book tells the stories of more than three hundred neighborhoods in twenty cities across North America and describes the building blocks that residents in these neighborhoods used in handmade ways to make things better locally. The building blocks they used came to be known as *assets.* Since the publication of that book and the establishment of the Asset-Based Community Development Institute to share the lessons learned from those communities, ABCD approaches have sprung up in many parts of the world. But in truth, all the book does is make visible what regular people do together to create a Good Life. In that sense, ABCD is simply a description of what people have been doing together for generations to make life better.

Three decades on it is clear that the assets featured in The Green Book are not unique to North America. They are found in every neighborhood around the world, to one degree or another, if we search them out and lift them up.

When *Building Communities from the Inside Out* was written, more than two decades of massive economic shifts had already blighted many cities in the United States and in other industrialized countries around the world. That trend has continued at pace up to today. Responding to this very real cultural and economic crisis, McKnight and his coauthor, John P. Kretzmann, argued for an alternative path toward a better future for such neighborhoods—a path of capacity-focused development. Policies and activities based on the capacities, skills, and assets of lower-income people and their neighborhoods became the new starting point. At the time, the traditional approach to development was a deficiency model focused exclusively on individual and community needs, deficits, and problems. Although the traditional approach remains dominant and commands the vast majority of governments' financial and human resources, some amazing green ABCD shoots are blossoming at the edges of various urban and rural neighborhoods around the world.

These outlier neighborhoods are reversing trends toward deficit-driven development and are instead committing themselves to discovering the hidden treasures (capacities and assets) within their communities. Their approach is not, of course, the answer to all of the world's problems; there are no silver bullets here. But their commitment is essential to how we move forward as a species and is therefore foundational in building toward a preferred future together. This book tells their stories.

Neighborhoods as Units of Change

We see the neighborhood as the primary unit of change and as a critical starting point for any serious effort to improve the odds for people who have been dissatisfied with current models of development. For most people we know, ourselves included, making public change happen at world scale is not within reach. Although we know a few people who are doing a wonderful job of making change happen publicly at city or county scale—for example, many major cities around the world are doing excellent community-centered work—for most regular folks, the canvas of a city or county is too big and too remote to create a better life on. That doesn't mean that local efforts can't spread from one neighborhood to others; it simply means that when it comes to widespread participation, it's a good idea to change the world one neighborhood at a time, by finding out what people care about enough to act on close to their own doorsteps.

Discovering Health, Wealth, and Power in Our Neighborhoods

Stand at your window or on the street corner of your block. Survey your neighborhood. What can you see? The fronts of buildings, cars, people, domestic animals, some businesses perhaps?

Now, consider what you can't see: The skills, knowledge, passions, and experiences of neighbors whose names you don't recall or barely know. The informal clubs and groups that you are not a member of. The local institutions that contribute in small but important ways that you never hear about. The physical gems that lay hidden in the built and natural environment, yet to be discovered by you and many of your neighbors. The cultural treasures buried behind invitations you have never received.

You are now imagining the parts of your neighborhood that are currently invisible to you and to most of your neighbors. Although these treasures may be hidden, they are abundantly available because they are close at hand, there for the asking. What you are imagining is the Connected Community, and the health, wealth, and power of your neighborhood.

Health

Robert Putnam, in his groundbreaking publication *Bowling Alone,* notes that "if you belong to no groups but decide to join one, you cut your risk of dying over the next year in half."[3] Since his study in the early 2000s, the preponderance of research in other industrialized countries shows his basic findings on the health of Americans holds true around the world but the outlook appears to be getting ever more gloomy. Yes, in industrialized nations there are, in general terms, definite health improvements worth celebrating, but there are also massive disparities in health outcomes for black and brown communities, and increasing numbers of people in consumerist societies are reporting feeling worse than people in their age bracket would have a generation ago. These feelings are closely linked to social disconnectedness in that those who are least connected feel the worst and experience worsening health outcomes as they age.

As a result, more and more industrialized countries are recognizing that loneliness is one of their biggest challenges. Some have gone so far as to appoint government ministers for loneliness. One in five people in Canada is estimated to be lonely, and these figures are broadly on trend with other industrialized countries. A study by researchers at Brigham Young University in 2015 found the ill effects of loneliness are as bad as smoking fifteen cigarettes a day.[4] Echoing Putnam's findings, the Brigham study looked at more than three million participants and found that increased social connection is linked to a 50 percent reduced risk of premature death.

Wealth

Many of today's mainstream ideas about wealth have tremendous impact on our personal health and the well-being of local places. They mostly isolate us from one another in order to promote the idea of the "rugged individual" consumer. Modern economies say the following to us:

- Whatever you need can be purchased, including health and security (consumer economy).
- Things are of value only if they can be standardized and mass produced (industrial economy).

Mainstream economics cannot see the contribution potential of the marginalized. It sees people on the margins as broken and deficient, as needy, as not needed. When our money, time, and energy are "invested" in the consumer, industrial, and/or helping economies, we are often left separated from our neighbors and overly dependent on external sources of support at the expense of our neighborhood economies. In other words, investment in things outside our locality is sometimes a form of divestment from our community. It's a net loss. In the name of economic progress, our orthodox economic theories demand that we divest ourselves of time, energy, and creativity in our home community in favor of investing them elsewhere.

By contrast, the examples we share in this book feature the virtues of a neighborhood economy. We share stories about what Zita Cobb and her neighbors achieved on Fogo Island, and what Maria Lai and local villagers gave birth to in Ulassai in Sardinia. Such stories offer us a window into an alternative form of economy, a place-based, rooted economics that treats local culture, local ecology, and community capacities as sacred and as integral to all meaningful progress. In this book you will see that, contrary to popular opinion, when we shift from a scarcity mindset to an abundance mindset, it is possible to have our cake and eat it too.

Discovering the Source of Our Power

Who here has the power to make things happen? For many the answer is, *No one here has the power to produce meaningful change; if anything is going to change, it will be because someone from out there (government or its allied institutions) comes to change us. We must therefore use what little local power we do have to get them here.* These words convey the view that we draw our personal sense of power from the quality of the relationship between us and government.[5] When the relationship is unsatisfactory, people feel a loss of capacity to exert power over their lives and over those who govern them, so they grow apathetic or angry.

This is an interesting argument, with some merit, but it is an institutionalist view of society. There is another way of understanding a person's sense of power.

The anger we observe internationally grows significantly from the dissatisfaction that millions of people feel because they are locally disconnected from one another and sustainable livelihoods. In the absence of these connections, the necessary capacities to produce better outcomes in our neighborhoods and present a stronger voice to government fail to take root. The ABCD Institute emphasizes the tangible local *sources* of power that create a real sense of "agency"—the local relationships that make people feel powerful, connected, and satisfied. This book returns to these wellsprings and invites us to drink deeply. The quality of our shared future depends on it.

For each of the stories that you read in this book, millions more remain untold. These pages seek to honor all those regular folks who show up every day and through modest but consistent practices tap into a new form of power: community power. Community power increases the health, economic viability, care, environmental integrity, and child-raising capacities in neighborhoods and ensures that the fruit of the community's collective labor is supplemented by government supports once their business is done. They do these things without expectation of personal return or the intention of changing the world. Instead, they are guided and mobilized by a culture of contribution. They continue to be our most authentic teachers and our greatest hope as we chart a course toward an alternative, more satisfying future.

The Voorstad Neighborhood of Deventer, the Netherlands

That is exactly how community-driven change started in the Voorstad neighborhood of Deventer in the Netherlands. One day, Patrick and Leendert were sitting on deck chairs on the brick-paved footpath outside their front doors chatting with each other, as they did most days. The conversation turned to how harsh the environment of the street looked; they felt there were too many bricks and not enough plants and trees to soften the view. So they started digging up some of the bricks—just a few under their windows initially—to reveal the soil underneath. They then used the bricks they had dug up to create a boxlike border around the empty space and filled it with compost and some plants. And just like that they had a mini street garden.

They had no permission to do this and little concern about what, if any, trouble they might get into with city officials. The next day, as they assumed their usual positions on their deck chairs, some of their neighbors gathered to admire the new street gardens under their windows. Then a neighbor asked Patrick and Leendert to create a mini street garden for them. Both men were unemployed and had the time to do so; in fact, they were very happy to be asked. It did not take long at all before street gardens began popping up on both sides of their street, compliments of Patrick and Leendert. They barely had time to sit down, but they loved every minute of their newfound roles. Neighbors on other streets heard about the street gardens and requests started pouring in. Soon both men were mentoring others on even more streets on how to create mini street gardens.

One day, while speaking with a lady who was knitting on a chair outside her house, Patrick told her he had seen others also knitting and suggested connecting her with them. She liked the idea and so began the Voorstad knitting club. The members started by knitting scarves for the community-owned football club called the Go Ahead Eagles, which led to a Guinness World Records attempt to knit a scarf long enough to wrap around the entire neighborhood, as an outward demonstration of the warmth of their community.

Patrick and Leendert met many neighbors with wonderful ideas for improving their neighborhood. They would say things like, "I'd love to do X, if only there were three or four neighbors to help me." On nearly every occasion, these two amigos knew just the people to connect them with. One day, while speaking with parents about the absence of a playground in the neighborhood, Patrick and Leendert got them involved along with other neighbors in a mini treasure hunt to find an empty lot in the neighborhood. The parents discovered a perfect location and created their own playground, ably decorated with mini gardens.

With hundreds of mini street gardens, a three-kilometers-long scarf knitted by 185 people and wrapped around the neighborhood, and a playground—all handmade and homespun—it was now clear that something special was stirring up, something bigger than the sum of all these great initiatives: this disconnected neighborhood was becoming a Connected Community; the culture of this place was changing. In addition to individual initiatives springing up, new associations were also forming every other week. Patrick, Leendert, the knitting club, and the playground parents agreed that they would meet together with others from the neighborhood and with neighborhood leaders from the football club (the Go Ahead Eagles).

By the end of a day of storytelling, celebration, and envisioning, a number of new community initiatives had been planned. Two ideas that emerged that day will go down in local lore for many years to come. The first was to establish the Street Gardens Academy and appoint Patrick and Leendert as the directors so that they could feel proud of their achievements up to that point and show that they were authorized by their neighbors to mentor others in creating even more street gardens and playgrounds in the neighborhood. The second idea involved knitting a scarf to wrap around a home allocated in 2015 by a local housing company to a family who had fled Syria following the Syrian civil war that started in 2011.

When asked to explain why they wanted to wrap an entire house in a scarf, one neighbor summed it up as follows: "If we are serious about being a warm neighborhood here in Voorstad, then we must be willing to welcome strangers and be able to demonstrate that; what better way than to wrap the house of our newest neighbors in a scarf with the colors of our community football team, stitched by the hands of hundreds of their new neighbors?"

This book has been written at the feet of people like Patrick and Leendert and their neighbors. Drawing on similar stories from hundreds of neighborhoods in more than fifty countries around the world, we are humbled and privileged to share what they have taught us about the journey from the disconnected neighborhood to the Connected Community.

The Journey toward the Connected Community: Discover, Connect, Mobilize

We have organized the book to reflect the processes and shifts we have learned about by walking alongside these neighborhood community-building efforts. In line with three stages in a recurring process of change that connecting communities tend to follow—Discover, Connect, and Mobilize—the book is divided into three parts:

Part One: Discover (Chapters 1–3)

Part Two: Connect (Chapters 4–6)

Part Three: Mobilize (Chapters 7–9)

Each part of the book is a gentle call to action. In part 1, the call is to join with your neighbors in discovering what you care about enough to take collective action on, and then in discovering the assets that surround you that can be used in service of shared civic endeavor. The call to action in part 2 is an invitation to positively connect community energy and passions and the various local assets within the neighborhood. In part 3 you are invited to make manifest the assets you have discovered and connected with your neighbors.

Within these three parts, we share nine shifts that we regularly observed in the journey from the disconnected neighborhood to the Connected Community.

Part One: Discover

Chapter 1 is about *shifting our mindset.* In disconnected neighborhoods it is easy to overlook local resources and take the bait of the consumer story: your Good Life is in the marketplace. The Connected Community mindset, by contrast, prompts us to look first to what we already have before seeking external solutions. From there, against the backdrop of the various stresses of modern life, we explore ways of conserving time and energy to discover local possibilities and sustainable livelihoods. We call this process *homecoming.*

Chapter 2 is about *shifting from a deficit-based to an asset-based map.* The deficit-based map portrays the neighborhood as a glass half empty, with too many problems and deficits for local people to start creating a decent life together. By contrast, the asset-based map portrays the neighborhood as a glass half full, with enough assets to begin to create a decent life for everyone in the neighborhood.

Chapter 3 is about, where possible, *shifting to locally sourcing the ingredients we use to produce our well-being in place of pursuing costly, remote, and nonrenewable options.* This approach calls for a shift away from the contributions of individuals outside the neighborhood, remote institutions, external physical and economic exchanges, and consumer culture. We identify in their place six essential building blocks as more sustainable starting points for creating community health, wealth, and power: (1) the contributions of local residents, (2) the resources of local associations, (3) the support of local institutions, (4) the neighborhood's built and natural environments, (5) the local economy, and (6) local stories, shared heritage, and diverse cultural experiences. We recommend these combined building blocks as a first port of call if you are pursuing a satisfying and sustainable life for yourself and those you love.

Part Two: Connect

Chapter 4 is about *shifting away from overreliance on external and internal leaders and toward connectors and the art of connectorship, that is, the art of being a connector.* Traditional views of development place the responsibility for change on the shoulders of leaders. It is commonly assumed in neighborhood planning and development circles that the engagement challenge at hand is (1) to get external leaders to get their act together and/ or (2) to find residents with leadership capacity and provide them with the necessary training to improve their personal influence and impact. The traditional battle cry is, *Leaders are the answer.* In shifting toward Connected Communities, the growth challenge, as we understand it, is to broaden local circles of participation and ensure that associational life deepens so that everyone can participate and contribute. Connectors are people essential to this inclusion challenge and to welcoming strangers at the edge. There is no battle cry or crusade here, simply a persistent and genuine invitation. This shift is about connectorship and connectors are vital to this effort.

Chapter 5 is about *shifting away from viewing our neighbors as apathetic about the neighborhood and toward recognizing that they are in fact waiting to be asked to contribute.* Here we push back against claims and generalizations about our neighbors being too selfish, too busy, too stressed, too distracted, or too apathetic to care about their neighbors and neighborhood. Using evidence from our community work, we demonstrate that, generally speaking, the reverse is true, that in fact our neighbors and their associations are more active than any one person can know, and many who are not yet active are waiting to be invited to contribute to the common good.

Chapter 6 is about *shifting away from seeing the underlying purpose of our neighborhoods as being containers of consumption and toward viewing them primarily as units of production and the stages on which local sustainability plays out.* Viewed through the scarcity lens of disconnection, we have no real shared purpose as neighbors. Our primary purpose is to individually consume as much of our natural resources as we can afford, or to advocate that institutions assume central functions in the areas of health, safety, raising our children, economic and ecological stewardship, care, and production of food regardless of environmental impact.

Viewed through the abundance lens of the Connected Community, our shared purpose as neighbors is to produce the common good by assuming vital functions in the areas of health, safety, raising our children, economic and ecological stewardship, care, and local production of nutritious food. While community-centred institutions extend and supplement those community functions.

Part Three: Mobilize

Chapter 7 is about *shifting away from focusing on global crisis and changing the world as your starting point and toward creating change in your own neighborhood with your neighbors.* Chapter 8 is about *shifting away from outside-in planning and service delivery and toward inside-out change and action.* Together these two chapters offer a detailed, practical guide for mobilizing community assets. Here we go beyond old development methods such as finding leaders, doing a needs assessment, writing a planning strategy or funding application, and lobbying for institutional reform. Over and above these, we show you practical ways of mobilizing within your neighborhood using the following methods: convening a circle of connectors, conducting learning conversations, asset mapping, community building, community dialogues, and parties/celebrations/hosting. These are not binary choices. We are suggesting a shift in starting place that increases morale and creates widespread participation of neighbors.

Chapter 9 is about *shifting neighborhood relationships with outside actors away from wholesale distrust or unhealthy dependence and toward mutual intent and useful alliances that will result in identifying and auditioning what we call Useful Outsiders.* Outside actors can include professionals, elected officials, and various leaders from external institutions who are working with external institutional agendas. Useful Outsiders seek to be of service to community life; they cheer on community alternatives and feature community capacities. They see neighborhoods as creative and productive places. By contrast, Unhelpful Outsiders seek to recruit clients to their services and programs and see neighborhoods as backwaters of problems and needs.

Nine Keys to the Good Life

At the end of each chapter we offer a key to the Good Life, by which we mean an insight into more satisfying and sustainable ways to achieve well-being. At the end of each of the first two parts of the book we also offer three practical tools you can use to discover and then connect in your neighborhood.

Are We Just Letting Governments off the Hook?

As the authors of this book, we continue to believe in a capacity-oriented, community-driven approach to most social and economic challenges and possibilities, because of everything both of us have seen in our work across thousands of neighborhoods around the world, not to mention our review of the historical record. Both our experience and history confirm that significant community development takes place only when local community people are committed to investing themselves and their resources in the effort. That is why Connected Communities are never built from the outside in. Having said that, we firmly believe the state has a vital role to play in supporting and supplementing community well-being.

But we are still left with the question, *What role do outside institutions play if communities are the primary investors in change?* A follow-up question is, *Are we just letting governments off the hook in terms of their responsibility to serve the public?*

Clearly, valuable outside support and assistance can and should be provided to neighborhoods by various institutions to (1) supplement community capacities, (2) do for communities (in a spirit of service) what they can't do for themselves, and (3) protect communities from outside actors that would do them harm if left to their own devices. We discuss this topic more in later chapters, but for now the point we're making is that when we assume that external institutions have the monopoly on all the best answers to issues of health, wealth, and power, we are heading toward major disappointment and setting up the professionals who work for those institutions to, at best, fail in our eyes and, at worst, burnout in their jobs. The harsh reality is that for most neighborhoods around the world, especially where inequity and structural racism are felt deepest, collective health, wealth, and power must start from within the community. We argue that this is true for most modern neighborhoods if they are to enjoy satisfying and sustainable outcomes. Put simply, there is work for communities to do, and if they do not do it, it will not get done. There simply is no proxy for community.

PART ONE

DISCOVER

The focus of this first section of the book is on the Discovery stage of community building. The first call to action is to Discover. We look at Discovery under three distinct headings:

- **Homecoming.** Chapter 1 is about shifting mindsets from consumerism to localism and cultivating practices that connect directly to the integrity and value of our communities.

- **The Hazards of the Wrong Map.** Chapter 2 is about shifting from a map of what's wrong to a map of what's strong.

- **The Neighborhood Treasure Hunt.** Chapter 3 identifies the six building blocks of community well-being.

Discover at a Glance

	The Disconnected Neighborhood	The Connected Community	Keys to the Good Life
	Definition: Prioritizes relationships outside the neighborhood, which separate neighbors from one another, and promotes individual survival over community well-being.	**Definition:** Nurtures neighborhood relationships that enable people to work together to create a Good Life.	**Definition:** Key lessons learned from neighborhoods on their journey toward deeper connection.
	Chapter 1 is about shifting our mindset.		
D I S C O V E R	*Disconnected* **Mindset:** Often overlooks local resources; takes the bait of the consumer story: Your Good Life is in the marketplace (externally focused).	*Connected* **Mindset:** Looks first to what you/we already have before seeking a market solution. Doesn't overlook local solutions (internally focused).	**Key #1:** The extent to which we personally flourish is tied to how much our neighbors and our neighborhoods are flourishing. Hence our Good Life is found in our communities and local economies, not in distant marketplaces.
	Chapter 2 is about shifting from a deficit- to an asset-based map.		
	Disconnected **Map:** Portrays the neighborhood as a glass half empty, with too many problems and deficits for local people to start creating a decent life together.	*Connected* **Map:** Portrays the neighborhood as a glass half full, with enough assets to begin to create a decent life for everyone in the neighborhood.	**Key #2:** Refuse to allow others to use maps of misery to define you. Define your course of Discovery by starting with what's strong and you'll get to what wrong in better shape to face life's inevitable challenges.

Discover at a Glance, _continued_		
The Disconnected Neighborhood	The Connected Community	Keys to the Good Life
Chapter 3 is about (where possible) locally sourcing the ingredients we use for our well-being in place of costly remote assets.		
Disconnected Ingredients: 1. Contributions of individuals outside the neighborhood. 2. Remote institutions. 3. Physical assets outside the neighborhood. 4. External economic exchanges. 5. Consumer culture.	_Connected_ Ingredients: 1. Contributions of residents. 2. Associations. 3. Local institutions. 4. Neighborhoods' built and natural environments. 5. Local economies, not financial exchanges. 6. Stories and local heritage.	Key #3: The Good Life is found "between" us and our neighbors, us and our ecology, us and our economy, us and our culture. The Good Life is like a good cake: before you can make it you've got to find the ingredients.

DISCOVER

CHAPTER 1

Homecoming

Rediscovering the Value of Community

From Consumerism to Localism

The Discovery stage starts with a question: *What is currently distracting us from searching more deeply and appreciating more fully the resources we need for a Good Life that we have close to home?* There are many possible answers to this question, but in this chapter we'd like to nominate consumerism as the main culprit, the number one distracter from the value of what surrounds us. Here's why: consumerism carries two related messages that dampen the impulse to discover hidden treasure in our own neighborhoods. These messages can be summarized as follows:

- Your Good Life is in the marketplace outside your neighborhood's economy, first to be bought and then to be consumed.
- Local handmade and homemade solutions are not enough.

So the goods and services outside our communities, which can be packaged and purchased, are valued while local assets are subtly devalued. The difficulty here is that we pursue the things we value. That's why our first step toward discovering what we have locally is to reverse the emphasis that consumer culture places on shop-bought alternatives to local assets. Here's an anecdote to further illustrate this point.

John, one of the authors of this book, loves to visit the West of Ireland. When he travels there, he rents a little house near a lake. He enjoys fishing and so travels with an easily assembled fishing rod. On one occasion he didn't have any bait, so he went to a little store in the local village and asked the gentleman there, "Do you have any bait?" The shopkeeper replied, "What do you mean by 'bait'?" "Well," John said, "like worms."

The shopkeeper looked surprised. He said, "On your way into my shop, did you see those two big whitewashed stones at each side of the door you walked through? Well, if you go out there and turn one of them over, you'll find a lot of worms; they'll provide all the bait you need."

This story offers a great life lesson: for the most part (there are exceptions to every rule), all around us there is almost everything we are looking for if we're prepared to live within reasonable limits. That truth is hard to see if we think the way to have a Good Life is to buy it. That's why, if we are only consumers, we will never see what's there. To see what's there, we must be crafty: creators, makers, producers.

Looking First to What We Have Before Seeking a Market Solution

In every community, the worms are the equivalent of the hidden treasures in our neighbors and neighborhood. They can be found in the local soil (the place and relationships) if we're prepared to go digging to uncover them. The worms in this sense are what we need to live a vibrant and Good Life and to secure life's necessities.

In John's story, he took just enough worms, but not too many—an important reminder that in nature if you take too much you eventually destroy the ecology. The other important dimension of the story is that the shopkeeper did not try to sell John anything. This is an uncommon experience for modern consumers.

Before we enter the Discovery stage, we've got to ask, *Would our current values take us outside the shop to search beneath the whitewashed stones, or would they prompt us to get into our car and drive toward a better Main Street store with more product options?* The question is whether we take the bait and go shopping outside our local economies for our Good

Life, or whether our personal values allow us to create even a little space for the possibility that some primary pieces of the jigsaw that make up a decent life are found close to home in the neighborhoods that surround us. We tend to search out what we value. So, before we can fully set off on a journey of Discovery in our neighborhoods, the first and most obvious question to ask is, *Is there value in what's local?*[1]

Local Solutions in the Face of Global Challenges

In a world facing so many global crises, it is understandable to have doubts as to the power of local people to influence climate change, rising unemployment, economic challenges, and the ever-growing issues of loneliness and poor health. The dominant story is that local efforts don't amount to much; real change happens in faraway boardrooms, not around kitchen tables and local shorelines. The future of our local economies and built and natural environments relies on what happens on Wall Street; not on our street. Our welfare is in the "invisible hand" of the marketplace, not in the hands of hardworking local businesses and the neighbors who act as patrons to the local economy by choosing to "buy local." The same people who dismiss local economics also sneer at those engaged in the sharing economy, where, for example, car sharing in neighborhoods is chosen over car ownership. In this book we argue that the story that top-down big institutions are our best hope is half baked; that story is written on a promissory note that has bounced over and over again. It is a story that has run its course, and in doing so has run us and our planet into a brick wall.

But there is hope. Take climate change, for example. Much of the energy we use to light our communities, run our cars, heat our homes, and power our local businesses comes from giant, distant, toxic, and nonrenewable sources of energy. The very real alternative is for local place-based communities to plan, finance, and produce their own local, renewable energy that is reliable, safe, and sustainable, and to do it in ways that bring a net financial return back to the local economy.

This is exactly what people living on the Scottish Isle of Eigg did in 2008, when they became the first placed-based community in the world to go completely *off-grid*. Today they rely solely on wind, water, and solar power. They are truly a Connected Community. They are also part of a grassroots movement for change in responding to the global climate crisis, because they are adding a new possibility to the "Reduce, Reuse, and Recycle" call to action: Replace. They are replacing distant, polluting, nonrenewable sources of energy with community alternatives, and they are making honest money for their local communities while doing so, because they are getting paid for returning clean energy back to the mainstream grid.

We want to lift up the facts that so often get overlooked and invite you to consider your options with refreshed eyes. Year after year, labor market surveys in Great Britain show that people living in Connected Communities are four times more likely to find meaningful employment and build sustainable livelihoods through local networks than through a Job Center. Research on health highlights that people living in supportive communities increase their chances of being healthy by 27 percent. In his 2013 article in *New Scientist*, "When Disaster Strikes, It's the Survival of the Sociable," Robert Sampson, one of the world's most respected social scientists on policing and public safety, tells us what the evidence proves: "stronger neighborhoods have significantly less crime."[2]

And the virtues of localism don't stop there. When sufficiently enterprising, local communities can punch well above their weight, producing decent livelihoods and vibrant economies that are the envy of the world. Consider what is unfolding on Fogo Island in Newfoundland, Canada.

Fogo Island

By the early 1990s, after decades of intensive fishing, the northern cod stocks in Canada collapsed, dropping by more than 90 percent from 1962 to 1992. For the people of Fogo Island, Newfoundland, things changed drastically with this collapse of the fishing industry, the main employer on the Island. Facing a serious crisis and with little time to pivot, the community in Fogo staged a world-class comeback.

Zita Cobb is a central contributor to this Connected Community story. She grew up on Fogo Island with her seven brothers and her parents through the 1960s. Despite not having any running water or electricity until she was ten, she describes her childhood as idyllic and Fogo Island as her "salty Narnia" (referring to the fictional world portrayed by C. S. Lewis in his book series *The Chronicles of Narnia*).

Zita's father, who had a deep understanding of ecology, saw from the start the jeopardy in which the "monster ships" that fished day and night were placing Island life. The economic model these outsiders lived by, in which they turned fish into money, with no regard to nature, culture, community, or sustainability, cast an ominous shadow over Fogo Island's future. It was a mindset so utterly out of step with the Island's barter system of trading fish for other essential goods—a strong feature of the economic life of the Island right through the 1960s—that most locals simply could not get their heads around this insanity. Concerned that this grotesque approach to making money was going to destroy all he and his fellow Islanders loved, he encouraged Zita to study business and figure out how the money system worked. This is the story of her homecoming.

Honoring her father's wishes, Zita left Fogo Island in 1975 at the age of sixteen to study business at Carleton University in Ottawa, Ontario. Over the next twenty-six years she enjoyed meteoric success in the business world, ultimately becoming the chief financial officer of a major fiber optics company. Zita retired in 2001 to pursue her interest in philanthropy. With a finely attuned business mind, years of extensive experience, worldwide connections, and a deep love for Fogo Island, she turned her philanthropic attentions and personal gifts toward home shores. In 2003, she and her brothers Alan and Tony established the Shorefast Foundation, the aim of which is to build cultural and economic resilience on Fogo Island.

Up to this point, given that we've been challenging consumerism, you would be forgiven for thinking we are preaching anti-market economics. We are not anti-capitalism per se; we are, however, like Zita's father was, concerned about the damage caused when markets become dislocated from local nature, culture, and community and start to dominate communities, ultimately leading them toward collapse. The Shorefast Foundation set out to renew Fogo Island's economy in a profoundly different and better way, by re-embedding the marketplace in local culture and place.

Discovery Before Delivery

The Shorefast ethos is rooted in the belief that place, wherever it may be, is our most important gift. Respect for the integrity of place, culture, and community can be authentically achieved only by first committing to a deep period of Discovery. To deliver goods and services from the top down or to extract them from the outside in, with no regard for the visible and invisible assets of a place, is an act of desecration. Zita deeply understood this hazard, so before Shorefast delivered anything, they engaged in a patient process of making visible all the invisible assets and making valuable all those assets that were not yet sufficiently valued. The community-wide conversations invited Islanders to consider the following questions:

1. What do we know as a community?
2. What do we have as a community?
3. What do we love as a community?
4. What do we miss and what can we do about it?

These conversations happened at a pace that allowed trust to be built and were hosted in a way that lifted up that which was local, handmade, and homespun. Hospitality is naturally embroidered into the cultural fabric of Fogo Island life; the art of hosting has enabled the Island to maintain close-knit community connections over recent decades despite its economic challenges. In seeking to discover viable economic alternatives to fishing, the question *What do we know as a community?* was important because it illuminated something deeply valuable within Island culture that many Islanders took for granted. By shining a light on and appreciating its value, people were able to imagine ways of creating sustainable livelihoods through hospitality. It did not take much to go from there to answering the question, *How can we use what we have to secure what we need?*

In 2013, Shorefast built the Fogo Island Inn, a hotel now internationally renowned for its sustainable yet innovative design and all of whose operating profits are reinvested in Fogo Island through community projects and initiatives. Every part of the Inn, from its furniture to the food it serves, is locally sourced and produced, but with a clever twist. The Islanders are so confident in their own capacities and other local assets that they welcome design and innovation ideas from around the world.

You will see this over and over in the examples shared throughout this book. When you build community from the inside out in the ways we describe here, contrary to what some may assume, you don't create tribalism, you build resilience. This process includes willingness to welcome the stranger and to invite new ideas and intermediate technologies (simple and practical tools that can be purchased locally or constructed from resources that are available locally) that don't damage but rather enhance what can be created locally.

This level of openness was important because the next challenge was to attract the world to Fogo Island. Meeting that challenge is where the core principles identified by Shorefast shine through: deep respect for and commitment to local skills, crafts, and traditions combined with world-class architecture and design. Shorefast has created an offer that attracts quality ethical and sustainable investment from all over, then they reinvest surpluses into the local economy, ensuring that the money keeps circulating within the community and generating new opportunities.

Today, many members of the Fogo Island diaspora are coming home, enrolling in the local school, and investing in the shared future of their Island community. What's happening on Fogo Island is not about Zita or even about Shorefast. It is about Fogo Island and the inhabitants' willingness as a community to do what the shopkeeper told John to do in the first story of this chapter: Turn over the stones and you'll find all the bait you need.

In 2021, Zita became the first social entrepreneur to be inducted into the Canadian Business Hall of Fame, for the entrepreneurial elegance of Shorefast and the socially conscious business and philanthropy she stewarded through the Foundation.

Zita makes an important point when she says, "At the centre of a community is its economy. If there's no economy, there's no community." Her core gift is her ability to support people in discovering the hidden treasure that surrounds them and then turning that treasure into sustainable livelihoods.

We have had the privilege of meeting many people with values similar to Zita's and have visited other communities that have gone on journeys similar to that of the Fogo Islanders. If they could speak with one voice to share their values, we imagine they would say something like this:

> We are a part of this place, not apart from this place. We are not going to use it. We are going to co-thrive and co-create. We can live well as a part of this place if we do our part; we can't live in it if we exploit it, because to exploit this place is to exploit ourselves—we are one.

Neighborhood Economies

Connected Communities like Fogo Island and the Isle of Eigg have discovered viable local alternatives to industrialized, standardized, and exclusively knowledge-based economies. In this book we call those local alternatives *neighborhood economies.*

Neighborhood economies are founded on the following principles:

- Our common wealth is discovered on the day we and our neighbors agree we have important work to do and if we don't do it, it won't get done.

- Trust and cooperation between neighbors are what get the key job done.

- Our wealth is in our gifts—of people, place, and culture. We organize to spend our money in ways that create a circular economy, and we recognize that our current neighborhood economy is usually like a leaky bucket. If we're going to nurture our common wealth, we need to plug the holes through which our money is leaking out and disappearing into distant economies never to return.

Key to the Good Life #1: The extent to which we personally flourish is tied to how much our neighbors and our neighborhoods are flourishing. It turns out that we are our brothers', sisters', and planet's keepers. There is no such thing as self-reliance; we are all interdependent—which means our Good Life is found in our communities and local economies, not in distant marketplaces.

• • •

In this chapter, we lifted up the value of localism. Recognizing that one of the hidden dangers of consumer culture is that it sometimes baits us into overlooking local assets in favor of specialized external services or goods. And though local assets are not sufficient on their own to respond to all of life's challenges, they are essential to a decent, satisfying, and inclusive life. The Good Life starts close to home, when we discover what we have around us and the power we have within us as makers and producers. By adopting the mindset of a producer, a maker, and a creator, not a passive consumer, we learn to resist the gravitational pull of consumer culture and keep at least some energy in reserve to discover the gifts of our local places.

In chapter 2 we take another step on the path toward Discovery by considering what maps we are using to explore the territory and by shifting from deficit-based maps, which start and stay with what is wrong, and toward asset-based community maps that start with what's strong.

CHAPTER 2

The Hazards of the Wrong Map

From What's Wrong to What's Strong

As we go deeper into the Discovery stage, we invite you in this chapter to critically question the navigational tools you and your neighbors will use to discover your neighborhood. Whether we think of these tools as lenses, maps, or visions of our neighborhoods, what is clear is that, as we try to find our bearings in the Discovery stage, they have a huge influence on what we find or possibly overlook, and on whether we get stuck in the mud or chart our way forward.

Two Portraits

Neighborhoods are regularly portrayed in one of two ways:

1. Most frequently, the neighborhood is portrayed as a glass half empty, with too many problems and deficits for local people to start creating a decent life together.

2. The neighborhood is portrayed as a glass half full, with enough assets to begin to create a decent life for every resident when these assets are connected and shared equitably among all members.

The first portrait lures us up an alleyway in which all energy and hope are sapped; ultimately this is a dead end in terms of real change, because we cannot build a future on the half-empty part of the glass. The second portrait reveals the potential of the half-full part of the glass—the benefits of using what we have to secure what we need.

The Problem with Problems

Many neighborhoods have started to improve themselves by focusing on a particular problem. One of the reasons they have been successful is because they have not allowed the problem to own them or to blind them to other priorities and possibilities. On this point we can learn a lot from the residents of Montrose, a small town of fewer than eight thousand people in the outskirts of Melbourne, Australia. Nestled at the foot of a small mountain range, it is surrounded by native bushland and situated on the fringe of industrial and suburban areas, with a major arterial road running through it.

Our friend Chelsey Cooper, a member of the Montrose Township Group, tells how for decades a roundabout has enabled traffic to move relatively smoothly through the town. But when we met in 2017, government funding had been allocated to remove the roundabout, widen the road, and place stoplights in this intersection. Chelsey recalls, "There was no community consultation conducted before the decision was made, and many people were angry and scared" about what this change could do to their town. It had become the dominant focus in their community and was increasingly crowding out all other conversations.

The residents of Montrose needed time and space to work through their concerns and to organize their best collective response, but there was a growing sense among them that they also needed to hold space to work on other priorities. They recognized that they could do both. As the Irish poet Seamus Heaney put it in his 1984 poem "Terminus," "Two buckets were easier carried than one." Montrose Township Group triggered an alternative conversation: "Let's try to focus on what's strong about Montrose and not just what's wrong—and explore ways we can build on the assets we already have in our community."

Sometimes we can be so busy with the water being taken from one bucket that we forget to drink from and replenish the water in the other. We can do both. But the Montrose community went further: they decided to use what they had to secure what they wanted, and in so doing they shifted their starting point from the problem to possibilities.

They started by sharing stories with one another about what they were doing together that made their community a better place to live in. A clear theme emerged from those stories: they all felt that their community was at its best when they cared for and looked after one another. So many diverse examples emerged from their stories that they began to explore how they might build on them to help their community thrive.

Over a three-year period, they experienced a slow and steady shift in their collective focus toward building on their strengths and celebrating the stories that built on the culture of care and support they wanted in their town. Like many other communities around the world, they did this while facing enormous challenges: the COVID-19 pandemic, economic and social uncertainty, and fierce storms that left their community without power for days and damaged or destroyed many houses. It was not an easy time, yet they've still been able to maintain a focus on building and celebrating connections and community contributions.

It was this collective attitude that gave birth to the Montrose Giving Tree, a little tree that sits outside the local bakery. In the early days of the pandemic (when cloth masks were deemed adequate), one resident anonymously made masks and hung them on the tree for people to use if they needed them. Then more masks started appearing on the tree, as well as herbs, lemons, seeds, and other handmade goods. Today the tree has a homemade bunting, plenty of pegs on its little limbs for hanging things on, and two permanent wooden boxes where gifts can be left, all made by locals. People continually share their abundance with others, whether lemons, books, homemade teddy bears, lollipops, bubbles, flowers, and even handwritten notes of positivity.

These are gifts given by the community, and they boost spirits and inspire others to contribute too, whether by sharing a smile, an offer to help, or a handmade gift.

One comment recently made by a local resident sums up a deepening culture that is taking root there: "I have never known such a caring and friendly neighborhood as Montrose. I am one of the lucky ones."

If they had remained exclusively focused on the "bypass problem" and locked into the angst of the issue, they would never have discovered the depth of care and the abundance of support that they have in their township. The "problem focus" would have locked them into a mindset that, similar to the consumer mindset we discussed in chapter 1, would have caused them to overlook the invisible assets that surround them. The point here is not to ignore our problems or to assume a Pollyanna approach to real issues by focusing only on the positives. The point is, if you want to resolve a problem, you're going to need to be resourceful, and those resources are in the half-full, not the half-empty, part of the glass. Put another way, the people of Montrose use what's strong to address what's wrong and to make what is strong within their town even stronger. They don't ignore their problems, nor are they defined by them.

What about the Roundabout?

The story about the government's proposed removal of the roundabout has moved on quite a lot since we met Chelsey in 2017.

The arterial road has run through Montrose for decades, but the roundabout and the street's treescape have helped to maintain Montrose's village feel. The construction of a much wider intersection, the introduction of traffic lights, and the removal of mature trees threatened the character and safety of the town in the view of the residents. The local community organized an effective response and achieved significant concessions and general agreement on a compromised plan.

Although they will still lose their roundabout, the road will not be as wide as originally planned, and sixty of the trees that were to be cut down will be undisturbed. Additionally, the agency they are negotiating with is organizing a stakeholder group of representatives from the community to guide the landscape design and help maintain and enhance the character and village feel of the town.

The Traditional Approach to Development: Deficit-Based

The people of Montrose, like the residents of Fogo Island, found alternative solutions by looking at their community through an asset-based community lens from the inside out. For some neighbors, the negative portrait of their community becomes like a prison from which they feel they cannot break free on their own. They firmly believe their only hope is that someone from outside their neighborhood will come in to save the day. The harsh reality is that this rarely happens, and even when it does it hardly ever results in satisfying and sustainable solutions. Sadly, not only are residents of these neighborhoods looking out through the prison bars of this disabling portrait, but many outside actors are also looking in.

In community building, many institutions and communities follow a clear pattern that points out what's considered wrong, missing, and broken, then maps all these problems onto what's known as a *needs assessment*. For simplicity's sake, we can think of this assessment as an institutional map of our neighborhood. Using this map, which is drawn for institutions by expert "issues" mapmakers from outside the neighborhood, we are supposed to be able to figure out what is needed to correct the deficits. If this explanation makes no sense to you, don't worry. It's because it doesn't make any sense, in the same way that trying to write a shopping list (what we need) without first checking to see what's in our refrigerator and cupboards (what we have) makes no sense. People can't know what they need until they first know what they have.

Coalville: The Map Is Not the Territory

Such a map of deficits was produced for a former coal-mining community called Coalville (appropriately) in Leicestershire in England. Following the closure of Coalville's last four coal mines between 1984 and 1986, the community's economy and society were turned upside down. The residents' mental map of their neighborhood was transformed and so was the institutional and government map of the town, though both maps were considerably different from each other. The residents had a map of a vibrant community in their heads, but local government and institutions had a map of "issues" and deficits. For example, at a meeting with active residents, a senior staff member from one of the local municipalities said, "There is no community in Coalville."

The comment left residents who attended the meeting speechless, though not completely surprised. They had a lot of experience hearing people describe their town from this scarcity perspective. The habitual starting point of most conversations with or between government or institutional staff and residents was one perceived deficit or another. The makers of these deficit maps were secretly known as the "Isn't it awful? brigade." A few days after that comment was made, the residents who had met with the local government official suffered yet another dose of "Isn't it awful?" On this occasion, an arts charity that aimed to work locally but was struggling to "engage" residents boldly announced, "There are no creative people in Coalville." After these encounters, it seemed, at least to the residents on the receiving end of the comments, that the biggest problem Coalville residents faced was how they were viewed by some of those looking at them from the outside. These outsiders, mainly professionals, were not bad people, but their map of Coalville was not useful, and in many ways it was very harmful. This institutional deficits map was obscuring from vision all the assets that lay hidden in Coalville. But like cunning pirates, these savvy residents knew that this deficit map did not represent the territory they called home.

They were not alone. Most Coalville residents subjected to this map felt unseen and unheard. The map of deficits guided many outside institutions and their staff to the problem zones in Coalville. Institutional responses framed by this negative portrait became predictable. First, they would do a needs analysis, highlighting the deficits of Coalville, and then apply for funding to parachute more professionals into the area to address those perceived needs. Those new professionals would then in turn try their heroic best to fix, correct, advise, and rescue. This pattern happened over the course of a three-year cycle in which each project would take a year to set up, a year to "deliver," and then a year to wind down. Once funding ended, another needs assessment would be done to secure more funding to repeat that cycle. Little changed. More and more locals doubted the map, resented the three-year funding "spin cycle," and began to question the effectiveness of many institutional plans and professional interventions in the lives and incomes of local families.

As one resident asked, "Since the pits closed, how much money has gone to professionals paid to help us, and how much has gone to people living in poverty?"

Increasingly, local people were jaded and demoralized. It was tiring to watch what they called "higher-ups" doing change to them, and then to observe those higher-ups' efforts fail. Many of the frontline professionals were also burning out or just fed up. Whatever the problems may have been, they did not lie solely with the community of Coalville, or even with the practitioners trying to change things from the outside in. The biggest problem was the map rich with deficit data that guided institutional efforts and led to residents being misunderstood, the bigotry of low expectations, and the arrogant, misguided, and naive belief that the best solutions come from outside the community and from higher-ups. The belief that community development is best done from the outside in and by top-down agencies is a stubborn, wrongheaded one.

It seems obvious to us that putting people down does nothing to lift them up; yet the practice of defining a neighborhood by its perceived deficits has become the standard way of trying to help communities around the world.

Coalville's fortunes turned when residents replaced the deficit map with an alternative one: the Asset-Based Community Development map. One of the practical ways they did this was by creating a graphic street map to portray all the gifts they discovered when they interviewed neighbors on the main street and asked them what they'd like to contribute to their community. Their graphic is striking in that it shows the streetscape as well as people with speech bubbles coming out of their mouths. One person's speech bubble reads, "I worked *down't* pit and I tell amazing stories." Another said, "I'm a *camerado;* I look out for others." And one person was kind enough to share their vulnerability and their contribution, saying, "I battled with my mental health; I set up a cooperative."

The residents who went out on the streets to initiate these conversations with their neighbors flipped the usual narrative from an outside-in perspective to an inside-out view. They moved from mapping what's wrong locally to mapping what's strong.

Coalville residents' response to the asset-rich map of their community was to set up Coalville C.A.N. (Capacity Assets Networks), an association of associations. The message to their neighbors is clear: "Coalville C.A.N. is proud of our area and wants its spaces, places and people to develop and thrive. We, the community, have the strengths and skills needed to make this happen."

No one map can capture the entire territory of a neighborhood, be it positive or negative. But before a community can understand what it needs from outside, it must discover what it has inside. If we want to build sustainable communities, we ought to set our compass bearings in the direction of what's strong and follow a map that shows the location of those strengths. So, let's take a page from Coalville's and Montrose's books and commit to discovering our neighborhoods afresh.

Key to the Good Life #2: In the same way a child cannot easily flourish in the shadow of a parent who constantly puts them down, a neighborhood can't hope to prosper in the shade of a map that defines them only by the sum of their problems. So peel off the labels that obscure your gifts and those of the places you call home. Refuse to allow others to use maps of misery to define you. Define your course of Discovery by starting with what's strong, and you'll be in better shape to face life's inevitable challenges.

● ● ●

The residents of Coalville and Montrose call our attention to the importance of being explicit about how we map ourselves and how others map
and define us. But perhaps in truth there is no map, positive or negative,
that can point us toward the so-called "promised land." The best we can
hope for is a compass that helps us find our bearings as we search out the
hidden treasures essential to creating a decent life for ourselves and those
we love. The next chapter reveals those hidden treasures in the form of
six assets that are available in abundance in every neighborhood when
we shift our frame of reference from deficits-based to assets-based community thinking and practice.

CHAPTER 3

The Neighborhood Treasure Hunt

Basic Building Blocks

Having avoided the pitfalls of consumer culture and taken care to ensure that we frame the territory in holistic and useful ways, it becomes much easier to discover the basic building blocks of our neighborhoods. In this last chapter in Part One, on the Discovery stage, we detail the hidden treasure that is in every single neighborhood without exception.

The six building blocks are as follows:

1. The contributions of residents
2. The capacities and other resources of associations
3. The community-building supports of local institutions
4. The built and natural environments of local places
5. Economic and other forms of exchange
6. Stories, shared heritage, and cultural diversity

Discovering the Hidden Treasure: A Story

Let's start our treasure hunt for these building blocks with a story.

Mrs. Lane's daughter, Jasmine, recently became a teenager. During Jasmine's summer vacation, she had very little to do. Her mom worried that Jasmine was beginning to go down what she described as "the wrong path." She was staying out later and had been seen by a neighbor talking to some kids who a few weeks previously had beat up a friend of Jasmine's. Mrs. Lane felt a strong urge to step in and do something to create "an alternative path" for her daughter. Once she got Jasmine onside, by reassuring her that she wanted to work with her to make the summer vacation one she would never forget, it was game on!

Mrs. Lane and her neighbor knew six other mothers with teenage daughters who lived on the block and the girls knew other girls their age, so they invited them all to a gathering at Mrs. Lane's apartment, where lots of ideas were proposed and discussed. As a result of that conversation, they (the moms and daughters) formed a team to organize a summer of activities with all the teenage girls on the block.

At the top of the girls' priority list were the creative arts, but the activities had to be with folks who would "get them" and who were into what they were into. Their mothers knew there were quite a few neighbors with artistic talents. They talked to these neighbors and found that almost all of them were willing to share their artistic methods with the girls. Because there were so many girls, a place was needed for them to get together with the local artists. So the mothers contacted Mr. Charles, who managed the local park, and he agreed to let them use a room in the building where he worked.

The organizing moms who prompted the summer initiatives agreed to a schedule to take turns attending activities; they also encouraged the neighbors who were sharing their talents to pair up and not work alone. They particularly encouraged pairings between neighbors who were great at featuring the girls' talents but not arty themselves and folks who were very artistic.

Over that summer, each of the artists spent at least a day with the girls, and some of the girls continued to learn from and work with the artists when the summer was over.

The second thing the mothers did was arrange to take the girls to visit the workplaces of some of their neighbors, including a large insurance company, a bank, a bakery, an accounting firm, and a beauty therapy school. This activity made a profound impression on the girls, tipping the scales away from the negative picture that many of the girls had internalized about their neighbors and their neighborhood and toward an alternative image of their community as a place abundant with the gifts of decent, productive adults who care about them and are cheering them on.

Finally, the mothers and girls decided to do a project to improve the block. The girls worked with all willing neighbors, on land and online, to create a family flag or door decal for each household. Nearly all of the households participated. They asked each family to identify some symbols related to themselves and their history that could be used on the family's flag, and they collaborated with the local history group to design each flag. Then they brought in a local seamstress and a designer who were members of the "knit and natter" group to create a flag or decal for each household. On one Saturday morning, all the neighbors gathered and hung their flags and displayed their decals. Then everyone walked from home to home learning about the families who surrounded them.

Mrs. Lane said of the summer's activities, "We broke the lines between the mothers. We broke the lines between the girls. We broke the lines between the mothers and the girls. We are a real community now." Her daughter said her mom was right; it was a summer she would never forget, and she was not alone.

At the end of that summer, the mothers decided to expand their team to include men. This extended team took on neighborhood initiatives that reached beyond working with girls.

Mrs. Lane's story involved using her community-building talent to create an association of mothers. Simply put, everything that happened to create a community in that neighborhood primarily involved connecting four local assets: individual talents, an association, a physical asset in the shape of the park, and a local institution, namely, the City Government, which enabled access to the park. No outside resources were needed. They also tapped into the assets of the built and natural environments and the local economy, not to mention local heritage and cultures. In all, they discovered, connected, and mobilized six basic building blocks, or ingredients, necessary to help a neighborhood begin the dance of nurturing a more connected and productive community. Let's look at each of these ingredients in detail.

The Six Building Blocks of a Connected Community

Contributions of Residents

The first building block is the *contributions of residents*, including the gifts, skills, passions, experience, and knowledge that residents contribute to the collective well-being of the neighborhood. *Gifts* are innate talents that people are born with and are happy to share. *Skills* are what people have learned to do and know well enough that they could teach a neighbor for free. *Passions* are what people care enough about to act on even though they may not always have a particular talent to bring to the issue; they care enough to act regardless. *Experience* is what people have lived through and have come out the other side of. *Knowledge* is what people know well enough that they can share what they know with their neighbors and/or the neighborhood's children.

This building block is evident throughout Mrs. Lane and Jasmine's story, such as in the generosity of the artists.

Associations

The second building block is *associations,* also known as clubs, groups, small local organizations run by their membership, and networks of un-paid citizens, who create the vision and implement the actions required to make their vision come true. Associations can be formal, such as a neighborhood organization, or informal, such as a book club or dog walkers who meet casually in the local park. *Association* is the collective word for *citizen*. Associations are where individual residents' gifts can be amplified and multiplied, as happens when individual musicians form a band.

This ingredient of Connected Communities is baked into the story about Mrs. Lane and Jasmine through the members of the knit and nat-ter group who participated and through the history club members who researched neighbors' family trees.

Associations are small face-to-face groups in which the members de-cide the direction and do the work to get there. An association of such face-to-face groups within a neighborhood offers an excellent platform for growing local participation and power from the inside out. There are various types of associations. Some are very formal, with elected officers and members who pay dues and operate according to a constitution; others are very informal, without a name or formal officers or members. Some are faith communities. Some are organized to address pressing social issues, such as a neighborhood crime watch group. Other associations are organized around sports, gender, arts, culture, age, or special skills and interests. Finally, some associations are organized on the basis of physical proximity, such as block clubs and neighborhood improvement groups.

The primary work and functions of all these associations are performed by local residents on a voluntary and consensual basis. In other words, the members decide what their priorities are and how they want to invest their time, energy, and resources.

What Do Local Associations Do? Local associations contribute to community building in three ways:

1. *They reach a large number of people.* Local associations can involve many more people in local action than institutions can. Their combined membership often represents a majority of people in the neighborhood and can therefore greatly influence and amplify new information relevant to the community, as well as encourage a wide number of residents to engage in community action.

2. *They shape members' attitudes and behaviors.* Associations are one of the most powerful forums available in society for shaping local culture. They establish norms and provide social incentives for new forms of community action. Small groups are also where people have their values reinforced or challenged, where we are most likely to reconsider and even change some behaviors. We saw this happen around sexual health behaviors among young men in Kibera, Nairobi, when the burial society, an association that nearly everybody there joins, began talking about the facts around the spread of AIDS and HIV. Associations also offer some modest insulation against extremism and polarization.

3. *They mobilize members to act on many different issues.* As we discuss in chapter 6, though an association may be focused on one particular function, it tends in practice to take on multiple functions that

reach beyond its primary purpose. For example, a seniors group may welcome newcomers, a food growers association may adopt public land and care for it, and a church group may start community organizing. In many neighborhoods, a great deal of community improvements are the direct or indirect result of the efforts of local associations.

An Association of Associations. Widespread participation of the kind described in the story that started with Mrs. Lane and her daughter cannot be achieved through randomly selected or self-selected people attending meetings, but neither can every resident attend every meeting. So, *how can neighborhoods better organize from the inside out for full participation and genuine inclusion of everyone's gifts and collective power?* We believe they can begin to move closer to broad-based, diverse, and inclusive participation when they work toward organizing an association of associations. With an association of associations, neighborhoods get the double benefit of a broader range of interests and a greater number of residents and their associations in the mix of multiple overlapping community conversations. That's what started to happen in Mrs. Lane's story : the initial group broadened their circle of participation to include dads and boys and began to blend into other neighborhood priorities.

An association of associations is not a "talk shop" or a one-stop shop where every issue becomes centralized and every group in the neighborhood is expected to join in or agree on everything. It is in fact the opposite. An association of associations is dynamic and based on trust and culture making. It therefore requires careful connectorship to nurture ties that bind but do not restrict people's ability to come and go. An effective association of these face-to-face neighborhood groups gives each group enough space to learn and grow while providing opportunities to do together the things they cannot do alone.

Local Institutions

The third building block is *local institutions*—groups of people who, unlike associations, work together for pay. Whether they are for-profit businesses, nonprofit or nongovernmental organizations (NGOs), or governmental institutions, they show up in the civic realm in either a community-oriented or an institutionally oriented way—that is, either facing and concerned about the community or facing and concerned about their institutions. An institution that is community-oriented acts as a resource toward community well-being and aims to be supportive, not directive. The goal of such supportive institutions is to enable citizenship and interdependence to be at the center of community life. They accomplish this by doing the following:

- Organizing their supports the way people organize their lives: small and local
- Putting institutional assets at the service of neighborhood community-building efforts and investing in alternatives to their traditional ways of working
- Being clear about what they are not going to do to/for/with neighborhoods, because doing these things would take power away from the people they serve
- In the case of government institutions, creating a dome of protection, in the form of bylaws and relevant regulations, against outside forces that could harm community life in the neighborhood

Again we can see this building block in the Mrs. Lane story, when Mr. Charles, the park manager, made available a room where the girls could do their activities over the summer.

Local Places

The fourth building block is the built and natural environments of *local places,* which are the main stage on which the first three building blocks become visible. As well as providing an ideal context for gift exchange, hospitality, and revealing abundance, locally bounded places are replete with all manner of practical resources that are essential to community life in a neighborhood. From the air we breathe to the community gardens we tend to the places where we casually bump into our neighbors or gather and engage in forming deeper connections, our shared places in the neighborhood root our community experiences. The scale of the neighborhood has the same positive effect on those relationships that a greenhouse has on tomatoes. In Mrs. Lane and Jasmine's story, the park was such an important physical asset to the girls.

Exchange

The fifth building block is *exchange*. When Mrs. Lane and the other mothers created a bridge between their daughters' career aspirations and productive adults in their neighborhood by giving the girls the opportunity to go to work with their neighbors for a day, they provided their daughters with an invaluable window into the economic exchanges of their neighborhood.

In the nonmonetary world there are three forms of exchange:

1. The exchange of intangibles
2. The exchange of tangibles
3. The use of alternative currencies

Exchanging intangibles. Throughout the long history of human exchange between kin, clan, and neighbors, exchanges have primarily been about the circulation of gifts. It is said that a gift is not a gift until it is given; it is also true that a gift is not a gift until it is received. That is why Connected Communities nurture a culture of giving and receiving, otherwise known as *reciprocity:* their exchanges are relational, not transactional.

Exchanging tangibles. This form of exchange involves the bartering or swapping of tangible resources. A favorite example of economists is a pig for five chickens; a more relatable example is the sharing of a lawnmower between six households on a street, or the setting up of mini libraries, where folks can leave books they've already read for their neighbors to enjoy. Another initiative we really like is the shared refrigerator, where food can be left for neighbors to take as they need.

Alternative currencies. In the mainstream economy, alternative currencies can be either tangible or digital. Prepaid phone cards and smart cards are examples of tangible alternative currencies, while cryptocurrencies such as Bitcoin, Zcash, and Ethereum are examples of digital alternative currencies. Communities can also create their own alternative currencies, enabling local choice and control. A popular modern example of an alternative to standard currencies such as the dollar (now known as *fiat currency* because it is backed by the government that issues it rather than by a physical commodity such as gold) is TimeBanking, started by Edgar Cahn in the 1980s. Members of a TimeBank use their time as a form of currency. Each hour of contribution is equal to all other hours regardless of what is contributed. It's a medium of exchange that rewards efforts to build strong, resilient communities. Another example of alternative currencies is England's Brixton Pound, an alternative to the British pound that can be used locally among participating vendors and individuals as a way of promoting consumer loyalty and a circular economy.

All three types of exchange—tangible, intangible, and alternative currencies—occur within and strengthen communities in that they increase gift exchange and deepen associational life. Most important is that they encourage shopping locally and other ways of investing in the local economy. Another positive relational spin-off from such exchanges is that they encourage hospitality; after all, gifts are best shared over nice food and in a friendly atmosphere.

Another form of currency exchange is based on "official" or fiat money. When kept local, such money exchange can play a powerful hand in nurturing community well-being in a neighborhood. Credit unions, worker-owned cooperatives, and shop-local initiatives are all good examples of this kind of exchange.

As lack of sufficient green buildings, intensive farming, and unsustainable modes of transport continue to bring our planet to the brink of extinction, it will be the sharing economy, the "Internet of things," and local cooperative models that will restore hope. The sharing economy is the only credible way forward, and increasingly the economics of the sharing economy—from car sharing to circular economic arrangements, blockchain innovation, and upcycling, which prevents "things" from reaching the landfill and instead allows them to enjoy several additional life cycles—will become the new normal. It is exciting to consider that new forms of intermediate technology that people are carrying around in their mobile phones enable this new sharing economy revolution to be produced by the masses.

Local Stories

The sixth building block of Connected Communities is *local stories*. Stories enable community well-being to flourish in neighborhoods. You can easily test this idea by considering whether you can think of any stories about a time neighbors joined together to make things better where you live. Shining a light on such stories and on community events is a powerful way to shift a local conversation away from what's wrong and toward building on what's strong. A culture of connectedness is fostered through story sharing. The sum of the adaptation of such stories over time is known as *culture:* local cuisine, art, beliefs, language, customs, and so forth. Culture finds voice through stories. We are all creatures of narrative and, when we cooperate, every conversation with our neighbors is the beginning, middle, or end of a story. It is in creating and exchanging stories that respect our own traditions and the diverse traditions of our neighbors that we ensure that our culture, "our way," prevails while respecting the multiplicity of other cultures and perspectives that coexist. Stories further enable us to pass on important life lessons and traditions to future generations. For the girls in the story that opens this chapter, this sixth ingredient was the icing on the cake, because not only did they hear a million neighborhood stories, but they were also part of creating a new story, one that says, "We are a neighborhood that takes seriously the adage, 'It takes a village to raise a child,' and we've done something about it—here's our story."

Key to the Good Life #3: Some say that happiness comes from within. Nature teaches us that many of our most satisfying moments in life come from "between," not within—between us and our neighbors, us and our ecology, us and our economy, us and our culture. The Good Life is like a cake. It has ingredients that must be identified and added in just the right amount to create a life that nourishes and sustains us.

* * *

The Unique Characteristics of Community Ingredients

These six building blocks are universal, useful, and simple to discover if we search while looking through the asset-based lens. *X* marks the spot of this hidden treasure, and the spot is our neighborhood. Mrs. Lane could have tried to resolve her concerns with her daughter at city scale, but in doing so she would have overlooked all six of these assets, and if she tried to resolve matters on her own or just on her street, she would have lost out on much needed support. The neighborhood was the perfect scale, the ideal unit of change.

The whole of these community ingredients is greater than the sum of its individual parts. Each of the six building blocks are interdependent. When one is weakened, all are affected. There is no shop-bought alternative that can lead to more sustainable or satisfying outcomes. Jasmine could have been placed in an institutional alternative to the community summer program, but at what price? Consider all that would have been overlooked and all the priceless experiences the girls and their neighbors would have missed out on.

In the next chapter, the beginning of Part Two, we look more closely at people like Mrs. Lane and her neighbors, who managed to connect so elegantly the building blocks of their neighborhood in addressing their daughters' needs.

Three Tools for Discovery

Tool 1: Gifts of the Head, Heart, Hands, and Conscience

As an alternative to having a traditional meeting, why not try having conversations with the members of your group to discover more about them as individuals and what they would like to contribute to the neighborhood. The following exercise, called Gifts of the Head, Heart, Hands, and Conscience, is a very gentle way of doing that. Try pairing up and having one-to-one conversations in which you share with each other the following gifts:

Gifts of the Head. These are things that neighbors know, such as knowledge about local history or local flora and fauna. Other neighbors could be strong at reflection or discernment, having the ability to weigh facts and diverse perspectives and reach wise judgments in a way that includes others.

Gifts of the Heart. These gifts are emotional traits that individual neighbors possess and share willingly, such as empathy and warmth, caring for people at the margins, and natural affection for and kinship feelings toward others. This gift domain includes people with relational know-how, who are good at peacemaking, healing, bridge-building, and understanding group dynamics and unspoken emotions.

Gifts of the Hands. These gifts are talents—such as cooking, gardening, playing a musical instrument—in which individual neighbors are proficient enough to teach them to other neighbors or support their neighbors in developing. People with gifts in this domain are of a practical disposition and in touch with their surroundings—their hands are "in the soil."

Gifts of Conscience. These gifts are principles of fairness and social justice. They are the ideals and values that a neighbor is prepared to stand up for and to step out from the crowd to stand by, such as taking affirmative stances in relation to racial equity, gender equality, inclusion, and economic justice. Gifts in this domain are related to courage, integrity, solidarity, and commitment.

As a pair, take fifteen minutes each to share with each other what gifts you believe you have. After thirty minutes of sharing, return to the group, sit together, and present the person you interviewed to the group by identifying their gifts. Once all the gifts are shared, discuss ways you could be more gift conscious as a group. If you enjoy the exercise, encourage other groups in the neighborhood to give it a go.

Tool 2: The We Can Game

The We Can Game is a fun card game that people of all ages can play. It allows them to discover their neighbors' skills in a nonthreatening, playful way. The game uses a deck of one hundred cards, each with one practical skill, such as "making jam," on it. As each card is turned up, the players are asked to nominate in which of four piles the card should go:

1. We Can (as in someone in the group can do that)
2. We Can't but We Know Who Can
3. We Can't and We Don't Know Who Can
4. Who Else/What Else?

People are always amazed and delighted when they see how few, if any, cards go in the third pile.

The details of how to facilitate the game and where to download the cards can be found in Resource 1 at the back of the book.

Tool 3: Community Walk and Asset Mapping

Put out a call to interested neighbors to join a community walk on a set morning. You can involve schools, local faith communities, and sports clubs, or just start small with a handful of interested neighbors. Then allow the idea to ripple into future community walks that can involve more and more neighbors.

Try dividing up into smaller groups and visiting different parts of your neighborhood. Go on a treasure hunt to find all the invisible and visible, but not always valued, assets (building blocks) in your neighborhood. If helpful, you could use the six building blocks as a guide and simply sketch out the areas of your community that you plan to visit and keep a record of what you discover under those six headings.

Again, the six building blocks are as follows:

1. The contributions of residents

2. The capacities and other resources of associations

3. The community-building supports of local institutions

4. The built and natural environments of local places

5. Economic and other forms of exchange

6. Stories, shared heritage, and cultural diversity

Regroup at an agreed-upon time with the others who did the community walk and have fun sharing what you all discovered on your treasure hunt. Include some community artists, who will know what's needed when it comes to creating a portrait of what has been discovered. This walk is a great opportunity to include young children too. We have learned over the years not to suggest what material or methods people might use to create a map or portrait of their discoveries. Simply find materials and crafts that make the best sense in your context. Try sourcing local mediums, such as wool, pavement chalk, and so on. The most important thing to remember is to have fun. Another thing worth remembering is that the map captures just a small number of the treasures that are actually there to be discovered. Each time you do a community walk, the map will change.

PART TWO

CONNECT

The focus of this second part of the book is on the *Connecting* stage of community building. The second call to action is to *Connect*. We look at connecting under three distinct headings:

- **Connectorship.** Chapter 4 is about shifting away from an over-reliance on external and internal leaders and toward connectors and the art of connectorship.

- **Waiting to be Asked.** Chapter 5 is about shifting away from viewing our neighbors as apathetic about the neighborhood and toward recognizing that they are in fact waiting to be asked to contribute.

- **Units of Production.** Chapter 6 is about shifting away from seeing the underlying purpose of our neighborhoods as being containers of consumption and toward viewing them primarily as units of production and the stages on which local sustainability plays out.

Connect at a Glance

The Disconnected Neighborhood	The Connected Community	Keys to the Good Life
Definition: Prioritizes relationships outside the neighborhood, which separate neighbors from one another, and promotes individual survival over community well-being.	**Definition:** Nurtures neighborhood relationships that enable people to work together to create a Good Life.	**Definition:** Key lessons learned from neighborhoods on their journey toward deeper connection.
Chapter 4 is about shifting away from overreliance on leaders and toward connectors and connectorship.		
Disconnected **Responsibility:** The challenge is to get external leaders to get their act together, and to find residents with leadership capacity and provide them with the necessary training to improve their personal influence and impact. Leaders are the answer.	*Connected* **Responsibility:** The challenge is to broaden circles of participation and ensure that associational life deepens. Connectors are essential to this challenge and to welcoming strangers at the edge. This challenge is about connectorship.	**Key #4:** The great innovations in life are mostly not the result of very clever people inventing new and extraordinary things. More often than not they are the result of regular, savvy people connecting ordinary things in extraordinary ways.
Chapter 5 is about shifting away from viewing our neighbors as apathetic and toward seeing them as eager to contribute if asked.		
Disconnected **Attitude:** Our neighbors are too selfish, too busy, too stressed, too distracted, and too apathetic to care about their neighbors/ neighborhood.	*Connected* **Attitude:** Our neighbors and their associations are more active than any one person can know, and many who are not yet active are waiting to be invited to contribute to the common good.	**Key #5:** One of the best-kept secrets of modern life is that our neighbors are happy to contribute and receive gifts, but there's a catch: they are waiting to be asked. So, the Good Life cannot be achieved without an element of positive risk.

CONNECT

58

Connect at a Glance, *continued*

	The Disconnected Neighborhood	The Connected Community	Keys to the Good Life
	Chapter 6 is about shifting away from seeing our neighborhoods as units of consumption to seeing them as units of production.		
CONNECT	*Disconnected* **Purpose:** Our shared purpose as neighbors is to individually consume our common wealth by purchasing or by advocating that institutions assume essential functions in the areas of health, safety, raising our children, economic and ecological stewardship, care, and production of food that appeals to diverse personal preferences, regardless of environmental impact.	*Connected* **Purpose:** Our shared purpose as neighbors is to produce the common good by assuming essential functions in the areas of health, safety, raising our children, economic and ecological stewardship, care, and local carbon-neutral production of nutritious food.	**Key #6:** The purpose of a neighborhood is to create a context and the essentials for a Good Life to be had by all who live there. For that purpose to come into everyday reality, neighbors have to take on some functions that only neighbors and their associations can perform. It is through such collective actions that we discover our community powers.

CHAPTER 4

Beyond Leaders
toward Connectors

This is the first of three chapters that unpack the art of Connecting, which builds on the Discover stage of the journey toward the Connected Community. This chapter considers the question, *If the cavalry is not coming over the hill to save us, who takes responsibility for connecting people in our neighborhoods?*

A popular response to this question, especially in disconnected communities, is that external leaders need to get their act together and the community needs to find residents with leadership capacity. These leaders should then be provided with the necessary training to improve their personal influence and impact. In short, leaders are the answer.

We'd like to push back against that assumption here and propose an alternative response to the question of who is to be responsible for connecting people. The alternative to challenging external leaders and training potential resident leaders is to broaden the circles of participation within communities and ensure that associational life deepens. We believe, therefore, that *connectors* are essential to this challenge and are also the main welcomers of the strangers who are at the edge of every community. In short, connectors (in the context of what we term *connectorship*) are the answer.

Why Connect?

Before discussing the role of connectors, let's consider the value of con-necting in our neighborhoods. Knowing just six neighbors significantly enhances the mental health of each person and reduces the impacts of life's stressors, including significant events like the coronavirus pandemic.[1] This is one finding of a study that gathered views from people in Australia, the United States, and England. The report was spearheaded by an Austra-lian whose interest in the theme of loneliness inspired him to investigate connectedness and neighborliness as the antidotes to social isolation. The study also indicated that small acts of neighborliness have a positive effect on people's sense of connectedness.

Deeper connectedness makes social and medical sense, but making it happen requires more than random acts of kindness, though they too are important. As this international report on loneliness suggests, enduring connections to neighbors and place rely on acts of kindness and courage that are rooted in the culture of that neighborhood. Mrs. Lane and her neighbors understood this; to coin a phrase from her words, "Neighbors are not just for Christmas." A give, receive, and reciprocate social economy is the force that limits the advance of loneliness and its associated diseases. Crucially, good neighbors do not overstate their personal contributions to community well-being. Typically, they attribute the homey qualities of the neighborhood to the culture of the place. Such neighborly feeling is described as "just the way we do things around here."

In this chapter we are going to meet more people like Mrs. Lane so that we can understand what makes them tick and why we call them connectors.

Local and neighborly connections come in three main types:

1. *Individual to individual.* I want to talk to someone about cooking and someone else wants to join in: a conversation follows.

2. *Groups and associations formed by individuals.* A group of individ-ual neighbors want to play soccer on a regular basis: an association is created.

3. *An association of associations.* Some or even all of the associations in a neighborhood connect with other associations: an association of associations emerges.

Human connections can also take their shape from already existing neighborhood institutions, such as a local corner store or a weekly open-air farmers market where people from nearby farms sell their produce.

Neighborhood connections form in as many ways as there are people. Connections between residents can happen naturally, but they may also be created intentionally. Relationships can spring up seemingly out of nowhere, through a surprising or even a natural encounter, but they can also be created on purpose, through invitations. By cultivating the conditions in which connections are more likely to happen, neighbors can nurture and grow their connections with one another without defining what shape those connections ought to take or without defining what folks should do when they are connected. We call the people who nurture local relationships and who sustain the climate to generate relationships *connectors*.

The Gentle Power of Connectors

The hallmarks of neighborhood connectors are as follows:

- *Connectors are gift-minded.* Like bees to a flower, when they hear of a local violinist, resident connectors instantly know of a child who wants to learn to play a musical instrument.

- *Connectors are trusted by their neighbors.* Neighbors know that connectors are trying to join the dots in community and that they are not in it for themselves.

- *Connectors believe that their neighbors want to contribute to the well-being of their wider neighborhood and that what they need is an invitation.* As a result, connectors are happy to make offers and extend invitations that their neighbors can't refuse.

- *Connectors feel welcome to get involved in other people's "business."* They invite others into public (shared) efforts, or what some call "the commons," and they do so in a way that feels nonintrusive.

Not everybody in every neighborhood is a connector, but every neighborhood—from Edmonton in Canada to Edinburgh in Scotland, and your neighborhood—has connectors. If you are interested in nurturing a more connected neighborhood, it is essential to first find the connectors, and it is worth getting to know them. If you're reading this book, you may be one yourself. Finding the connectors is a bit like duck hunting: it requires the right duck call. Connectors have highly attuned senses and they tend not to respond to invitations like "Come to our meeting." They are equally unlikely to pay attention to flyers looking for volunteers. Connectors are more interested in an invitation to a party than to be part of a committee. They would be shocked to think of themselves as leaders in the traditional sense of that word, where leaders are at the front of the group galvanizing followers around key issues. Connectors avoid the front of a crowd, and they are allergic to polarizing issues, because they are focused on authentic connections.

One such person is Howard Lawrence, a resident of the Highlands neighborhood in Edmonton.

Connectors in Edmonton

In 2013, Howard decided to see if the ideas in *The Abundant Community* (2010), a book that John McKnight wrote with Peter Block, made sense. Howard started small, close to where he lived, guided by the simple belief that his neighbors have a lot to offer one another and, if invited, would be willing to contribute their capacities to improving the Highlands neighborhood.

With the help of some of his neighbors, and through hundreds of regular and repeated conversations, more and more residents got involved in working on their neighborhood, not just living in it. Since 2013, and with no promise of a Hollywood ending, together they have steadily grown their neighborhood's collective pride, inclusivity, and creativity. In doing so, they have increased their capabilities to work together toward the common good of their neighborhood. As assets have been connected and neighbors have formed new associations, they have witnessed a rise in neighborliness and a deeper sense of well-being.

As Howard points out, there are so many ways in which neighbors can be supportive of one another. "Even choir—there are so many people in our neighborhood who want to sing in a choir but don't want to drive to join a choir. They would be happy not only to share the interest but, more importantly, build relationships locally."

Some folks at the City Government of Edmonton had their heads turned by what they witnessed in the Highlands neighborhood and by Howard's enthusiasm for the approach—so much so that they decided to support similar ABCD approaches in neighborhoods across the city. More and more neighborhoods are getting in on the action. Now, just a few years after the initial ABCD initiative started in the Highlands neighborhood, more than one hundred neighborhoods in the city are talking about, and many are also acting on, the idea of growing their neighborhood from the inside out, which has been profoundly influential within the civic realm and within the institutions of the city.

Why would a big institution like the City Government support such modest local steps? Well, aside from being bowled over by Howard's and his neighbors' passion, they recognized that such efforts improve public safety and health, increase inclusion, boost the local economy, reduce loneliness, and create new opportunities for neighborhood children and seniors, and they did so in ways that a city bureaucracy never could, no matter how hard they tried. In a practical sense, city officials could see the value of steeping back a little from business as usual to cheer on and create more space for neighborhood community building to grow from the inside out. They were learning to lead by stepping back and holding space for residents to step into the limelight.

Connectors in Edinburgh

The Village In The City initiative (VITC) in Edinburgh's West End neighborhood offers a fine example of this new style of leading by stepping back. Residents there call it *hosting*.

The initiators of VITC, Mark McKergow and his wife, Jenny Clarke, describe it as follows:

Village In The City helps you to build micro-local communities where you live. Whether it's at the level of a street, a few blocks, or a neighborhood, you can start and create your own "village in the city." The good news is it's not about money. It's about using your talents and taking small steps to engage your neighbors. And everyone has some useful skills, gifts and passions to bring to the service of our communities.

Mark and Jenny spent a lifetime working hard and enjoyed full and meaningful careers, but they missed the sense of community in their lives. Mark recalls, "We had friends in every part of the world, yet we knew nobody on our street."

The importance of having community in the neighborhood came home to them in 2020, in the early weeks of the pandemic lockdown. As proactive individuals, they decided to make full use of their extended time in their homeplace, which by then was the West End of Edinburgh, by establishing Village In The City.

Pre-lockdown, their neighborhood was alive with tourists visiting the West End for its bohemian vibes and cultural and entertainment offers, which are there in abundance. Above the storefronts and adjacent to the theaters, cinemas, and restaurants are the flats of local residents. In March 2020, the streets were eerily quiet as businesses shuttered their storefronts. It was against this backdrop of worry and uncertainty that Mark and Jenny entered into dialogue with their neighbors. Along with a few enthusiastic fellow residents, including Paul Hancock, they reached out with leaflet drops and on Facebook to ask other residents of the West End the following questions:

- Do you want to make your life and the lives of those around you better and more fulfilling?
- Do you want to build a better community on your street or in your neighborhood?
- Are you already involved in local community activities and want to share ideas and help others?
- Are you working from home and finding yourself wanting to enhance your locality?

The positive response was phenomenal. It seemed that there was a pent-up desire for a sense of "village life" in the city—and not just in Edinburgh but in neighborhoods in twenty-three other cities around the world.

The simplest way of describing the Edinburgh and Edmonton connectors' role in their neighborhood is that they are neighbors who know lots of other neighbors and want to do something to deepen and broaden these connections. Let us now examine the characteristics of a connector in more detail.

The Main Characteristics of Connectors

Most connectors are people with a special eye for the gifts, the potential, the interests, the skills, the experiences, and the capacities of their neighbors. They focus on those strengths and lift them up for that person and for others in the neighborhood. The vocabulary of connectors contains statements like "This is Charlie; he's got a great singing voice." Connectors go out of their way to introduce into community life those neighbors who are at risk of not having their gifts noticed or received, or who are at risk of being judged solely by their past or by their negative reputation. In Edinburgh, Mark, Jenny, and their fellow members of VITC think of themselves as hosts and take care to promote constructive conversations within their Village In The City, which is not always easy online but is a vital part of fostering inclusive and engaging community connections.

Crucially, connectors carry no hope or expectation of "fixing" the people with whom they interact. Connectors work on the principle that people are fundamentally decent and that the more connected they are in reciprocal relationships, the more decent they become.

Six main characteristics we have observed in connectors:

1. They invest their energy and vitality in the associational activity of the neighborhood, and because of these connections, they make a variety of further contacts quickly and easily. They may be connection brokers because they "know people who know other people." They enjoy belonging, involvement, connection, and reciprocity.

2. They achieve their ends because they are trusted by their community peers, not because of a position, title, or other claim to authority.

3. They constantly and publicly give credit to others. They spread the glow, find sparks to celebrate, and encourage people on to do even more, however modest it might be.

4. Connectors speak in personal terms; they say, "I'm a friend of your sister Mary and she said I should ask you about the choir you direct. I have a friend who loves to sing and has a beautiful voice who you might like to hear in your choir."

5. They are not apologetic, they do not beg, they do not ask for charity or help. Instead, connectors are enthusiastic about presenting the gifts of a neighbor to the hospitality of another person active in the neighborhood.

6. By their nature, connectors are sociable. They certainly are not lone wolves, but nor are they busy bodies. They have good boundaries and that's a big reason why they are trusted.

In our experience, connectors' belief in the hospitality of community is well-founded. Indeed, their confidence tends to grow as they find that there is broad community readiness to include people, especially those who have been excluded. Of course, not every person in every neighborhood is hospitable, but the vast majority are, and they are just waiting to be asked to participate (as we will see in the next chapter), and they are open and receptive to diversity. These are the members of the community they ask first, not the members who are negative, resistant, unwelcoming, or unsafe—although the hope is that a culture of care will spill out and start to spread into those hesitant spaces and resistant spots, warming those folks up to the possibility of an alternative future. Connectors know the terrain of hospitality and go with the energy, avoiding the pitfalls of rejection, or at least not taking it personally when they encounter them. The beauty of having the neighborhood as the stage and not just individual relationships is that you can move around and go with the energy as it ebbs and flows.

The Limits of Leadership

Having praised connectors throughout this chapter, it's important to ensure that we don't romanticize the role or substitute it for leadership. Connectors are not superheroes. We are emphasizing the value of starting with connectors rather than leaders not because there is anything wrong with leaders but because we are interested in connecting with everybody in the neighborhood, not just leading on issues.

It is important to recognize, though, that when leadership and the pursuit of leaders becomes the sole obsession driving neighborhood development, it deflects us from assuming personal responsibility and power as individual neighbors to act for the common good, and it permits us to place the responsibility of the many onto the shoulders of the few. As our friend Peter Kenyon, from Perth in Australia, jokes, "Many communities are like footie [Australian football] matches, where the players on the field, who least need the exercise, are doing all the hard work, while the spectators, who most need the exercise, are sitting down, telling the players what to do, and complaining when they don't succeed." Indeed, though the work of weaving our neighborhood connections can't be left to leaders alone, neither should we expect connectors to do all the work.

A Circle of Connectors

One of the very important functions that initiatives like Abundant Community Edmonton and Village In The City perform is that they provide a table around which connectors can gather together to work on connecting their neighborhood as a whole. A second and related function is that such initiatives pay close attention to ensuring that connectors who gather around that figurative or actual table reflect the diversity of the entire neighborhood and remain open and welcoming to the stranger. The work they do together is what we term *connectorship*.

What Is Connectorship?

Connectorship is an essential process that complements healthy styles of leadership with street-level relationship building, and it is this deep and wide local effort that leads to Connected Communities where everybody's contributions are invited and received. In that sense, connectorship influences the group life and culture of a neighborhood.

Key to the Good Life #4: The great innovations in life are mostly not the result of very clever people inventing new and extraordinary things. More often than not they are the result of regular, savvy people connecting ordinary things in extraordinary ways. In that sense, everyone can be an innovator if they just connect. So don't depend on a genius to invent a solution for you, or on a great leader to guide you toward the promised land. Believe instead that you have and you are enough when you are deeply and productively connected. Remember also that in every neighborhood there are individuals who are particularly gifted at the art of connecting. They deserve our appreciation and support.

• • •

Connectors are the individuals who enable us to more deeply and broadly connect what is disconnected in our neighborhoods. Connectorship is the way or means by which we do this. When a community's best connecting work is done, associational life in the neighborhood is deepened for everyone by everyone. A culture of kinship is the outcome of connectorship; it's what we refer to in this book as the Connected Community. Connectorship is the opposite of "tribalism." Instead of kinship circles made up of individuals who look like, vote like, and worship like us, such circles maintain permeability at the edges, with a permanent and hopeful welcome for the stranger. Connectorship is the antidote to modern echo chambers (online and on land) where we hear the sound of our own voices coming back at us to reinforce our biases and one-sided positions. Connectorship asserts our freedom of listening to others and not just our freedom of speech.

It is in the diversity of these new connections that tolerance and creativity can be found. As associations blend and mingle, the harsher edges of estrangement and fragmentation are smoothed out and we discover the "other" whom we feared is not a stranger but just a neighbor we have not yet met.

In the next chapter we show that, rather than being apathetic, our neighbors are much more willing to connect than we may assume, but they are waiting—waiting to be asked.

CHAPTER 5

The Community Is Waiting to Contribute

Neighborhoods present themselves in many guises. Urban neighborhoods with some level of infrastructure and planning have blocks and streets made up of various dwellings: apartments, flats, duplexes, condos, and so on. Rural towns and village neighborhoods are not just smaller in size; there can also often be great distances between dwellings and great variety in the size and look of people's homes. In neighborhoods like Kibera—the largest slum in Kenya, it sits on the edge of the capital city, Nairobi—the story is very different. Kibera's dwellings are precarious, and infrastructure and basic services are rudimentary; streets are pathways worn by human feet and can be washed away in heavy rains. In affluent cities, some of the marginalized and homeless are housed in formal and informal shelters, but there are those who die on the street due to the absence of shelter and exposure to the elements. There are kids hiding out in their friend's garage because of conflict at home, and others are living in crowded conditions, with two families living in dwellings barely adequate for one.

Amid all of this diversity of living arrangements, it is easy to suspect that the people in their various homes are as different as their homes and their surroundings. However, people are not as diverse as their material conditions suggest. In addition, whether people live in rich or poor, urban or rural neighborhoods, it may appear as if most residents are disconnected from one another and are not active in the community. Our experience of community building all over the world is that whatever the material conditions of a place, and whatever the appearance of community life, the outward appearance is not the reality. Most neighborhoods that present as broken and disconnected and that carry labels such as "disadvantaged" or "no-go zone" are in fact communities in disguise. What is not visible under the neighborhood guise is that most of the residents are waiting to contribute to one another's well-being and to the well-being of the neighborhood. Most residents do not see community as a committee or as meeting-structured connections, when and if they do experience it. If they judge community positively, it is because they experience it as warmth, connection, and celebration. Insofar as government bodies and institutions are obsessed with organization, management, structure, funding, and problems, then outside agencies and the communities "under the surface" of neighborhoods are invisible to each other.

In each of the stories we have shared so far, people were waiting. Their community gifts were disguised or invisible to institutions, to agencies, and even to most of their neighbors. But those gifts were present and awaiting the call to contribute and act. The call to action cannot be issued by a committee or a management plan; it comes best from a neighbor, from a connector, or from the associational life of the neighborhood.

Zita Cobb discovered that folks on Fogo Island, who were already incredibly active in responding to economic crises, were waiting to share even more. Her ask, framed in entrepreneurial terms, meant that folks could go even deeper.

The folks that hung the gifts on the Montrose Giving Tree and the people of Coalville moved from casual connections to connectorship because of thoughtful and intentional invitations from people they knew and trusted. You might say that, like Mrs. Lane's neighbors, all residents and neighbors are waiting to be asked, and some of them, once asked, will show up. How do you know that people are there waiting in your neighborhood? You don't, but we know that it is worthwhile to check to see if your neighbors too are waiting to be asked out "to dance." Our experience of most neighborhoods is that most residents are waiting for that invitation to the public life of your neighborhood, and that when you ask, you will discover a wide array of untapped assets just waiting to be discovered and then connected.

Let's get into some of the details of what we've been learning about various neighborhoods. For example, research in a low-income neighborhood in Chicago found that in seventeen randomly selected homes, the householders were willing to share more than 180 capacities. Specifically, they were asked to identify the following four kinds of capacities that they were willing to share with their neighbors and their neighbors' children:

1. The gifts they were born with

2. The skills they have learned

3. The passions they have acted on

4. The special knowledge they could teach their neighbors and/or their neighbors' children

It is important to acknowledge that there is a difference between someone saying they would in principle share a gift and that person following up on the promise in practice. The one-to-one conversations that unearthed these gifts hinged on finding out what people really cared about enough to act on. So, conversations that are intentional about those practical actions must tap into a resident's intrinsic motivation. People who are intrinsically motivated are more likely to act on their interests than those who are not. Conversations that aim to inspire action must not be about a shopping list of maybes: *maybe I could set up a childcare cooperative, maybe I could read to young people,* and so on. Everyone in community building has had experiences in which people have paid lip service to invitations and then the promises to show up and to participate have ended in empty rooms and personal disappointment. After a few experiences like that, your choice is to either give up or change tactics. The truth is that there is a knack to discovering what people are motivated enough to do that they will show up and contribute their gifts to the common good. Telling the difference between empty, well-intentioned promises and consensual commitment and passion is a vital skill in neighbor-level conversation and in community connection-building.

Although it is important to focus on discovering what neighbors care about enough to act on, what we see in Edmonton neighborhoods, for example, is a necessary willingness to go at at a pace that allows trust to be built. Residents there discover other residents' gifts, but then they are wise and gentle enough not to push people into action before they are ready. They take care to first build confidence and trust in one another and in their growing and deepening collective capacities. By taking the time to really get to know one another's gifts before they start to pair neighbors who are making offers with neighbors who are willing to receive, they have conversations that are not transactional (not one-sided or out to sell somebody something) and not aimed at taking something or forcing action from people. The conversations they have are called learning or relational conversations. Learning conversations help people to connect with their purpose and their passion. They start with a focus on possibility before they get into productivity. They start gently, with questions like *What could you share?* They then move on to such questions as *Of those five things, what would you most enjoy sharing?* Finally they ask something like *You mentioned you like Origami* [the art of paper folding in order to make things]. *If we meet others with a similar interest, either because they do origami or because they would like to learn how to do it, would you like us to connect you with them?*

This curious and attractive approach was used to bring to the surface the skills, passions, and knowledge that neighbors were willing to teach and to share, for free, in the seventeen randomly selected households in Chicago's Woodlawn neighborhood. The results were very revealing.

The seventeen residents of three blocks in Woodlawn identified 42 gifts, 49 skills, 53 passions, and 36 things they could teach. Details of each of these gifts, skills, passions, and "teachables" (things we know well enough to teach a neighbor for free) are in Resource Guide 2.

The tables in Resource 2 offer a window into a mostly undiscovered and disconnected set of possibilities in the Woodlawn neighborhood. They describe a gift bank that, if acted on, would serve as an enormous source of health, wealth, and power in the neighborhood. Such possibilities and powers are, to one degree or another, available in every neighborhood, in whatever shape that neighborhood comes. In contrast to the deficit maps that so many external institutions use to view the Woodlawn neighborhood, these tables offer clear evidence to create a new map, and the data allow the compilation of a sensitive and accurate inventory of neighborhood talent. This inventory shows that each interviewed householder averages ten capacities that they are willing to share. These capacities are typical of the unopened treasure chest in each household in every neighborhood.

To open the treasure chest and make visible the local riches, two actions are necessary:

1. Invite neighbors to contribute their abilities within the neighborhood.
2. Connect these abilities with other neighbors who find them useful.

Such connections are made in two ways:

- Neighbors who have capacities are connected with other neighbors who need those capacities.
- Neighbors with the same capacities and interests are connected to one another to form groups and associations on the block and across the wider neighborhood.

As both kinds of connections multiply, many new friendships are formed and the community begins to create a culture of contribution. This contribution culture manifests itself in feelings of belonging and mutual commitment that basically power a neighborhood's well-being.

So, in seventeen homes in this neighborhood, the residents are waiting to be invited to share their 180 gifts, skills, passions, and areas of knowledge. These potential exchanges require a neighbor or several neighbors to become block-level connectors who introduce people seeking gifts, skills, passions, and knowledge to other residents who can use or enjoy them. This brokerage or gift exchange process also ensures that several neighbors with similar capacities or interests are connected to one another. Examples of these gift exchanges include four families sharing childcare, five neighbors forming a daily walking club and improving their health while picking up litter, five neighbors concerned about the nearby polluted stream joining together to clean it up, and four musical neighbors forming a block band to play at neighborhood events. In each case, a new association was formed, making each individual feel more powerful while the new association creates neighborhood capacities to increase the well-being of all.

When the seventeen local neighbors were asked about their four capacities (skills, gifts, knowledge, and passions), they were also asked to identify the kinds of clubs, groups, organizations, and associations they belonged to or were associated with. Over the years, as we have walked alongside communities around the world, we have learned that adult residents of neighborhoods belong to or are associated, on average, with five different groups. So, on a block with thirty households, one can generally expect the householders to identify 150 associations. If fifty are duplicated, there remain 100 different associations with which neighbors are associated. Allowing for the associations that meet outside of their neighborhood, many of these associations represent significant local forms of collective activity. Such an abundance of associations and other forms of group life, as revealed in the Woodlawn survey, is the raw material that creates the productive infrastructure of a powerful neighborhood: the Connected Community.

In Spring Green, a community in southern Wisconsin, the nature of this infrastructure was made visible by four residents who conducted an inventory of the active associations of their rural town of sixteen hundred people. They were able to identify eighty locally focused associations. The local team of connectors interviewed the leaders of sixty-two of these eighty formal and informal associations. They identified all the functions and activities that each group performed and that contributed to the well-being of all the people in the town—what we think of as the "common good" of the town. The names of the sixty-two groups identified indicate the breadth of the interests of Spring Green's residents:

4PeteSake
American Legion Post 253
Badgerland Girl Scout Troop 2669
Bloomin' Buddies Garden Club
Bunco Babes
Christ Lutheran Church
Community Theater Association
Concerned Citizens of the River Valley

Cornerstone Church of Spring Green
Cub Scout Pack # 38 Spring Green
Driftless Area Book Club
Future Farmers of America
Friends of Governor Dodge State Park
Friends of the Lower Wisconsin Riverway (FLOW)
Friends of the Spring Green Community Library
Green Squared Building Association
Greenway Manor Volunteers
Habitat for Humanity
Knights of Columbus
Knitters at Nina's
Kops for Kids
Mew Haven, Inc.
Miracles on Hoof
Mostly Mondays Poetry Society
Older & Wiser Land Stewards (OWLS)
Pineland Association
River Valley Area Community Choir
River Valley Boosters Association
River Valley Mom's Group
River Valley Music Boosters
River Valley Players
River Valley Soccer Association
River Valley Stitchers
River Valley Youth Football Club
Rural Musicians Forum
River Valley High School Alumni Band
River Valley High School Madrigal Choir & Jazz Vocal Group
River Valley High School Senior Service Learning Class
Skills USA
Solstice Jazz Band
Spring Green Area Arts Coalition
Spring Green Area Chamber of Commerce

Spring Green Area EMT District

Spring Green Area Fire Protection District

Spring Green Area Historical Society

Spring Green Arts & Crafts Fair Committee

Spring Green Cemetery Association

Spring Green Community Church

Spring Green Community Food Pantry

Spring Green Dog Park

Spring Green Dolphins

Spring Green Farmers Market

Spring Green Film Club

Spring Green Golf Club

Spring Green Lions Club

Spring Green Literary Festival

Spring Green Senior Citizens Club

Stitch 'n' Bitch

Unity Chapel

Wyoming Valley School Cultural Arts Center

Although the names of many of these groups sound parochial and focused on benefitting only the members, nearly all of the groups were also engaged in activities that contribute to the well-being of nonmembers as well as the town as a whole. Associational names rarely tell us about the association's wider or spillover role in contributing to the common good. Indeed, its public work is usually invisible if one does not look behind the name. 4PeteSake, for example, raised funds to support their neighbor Pete in having a lifesaving medical procedure. Every other association in Spring Green supported their effort. The ethos in Spring Green is, *If you see a need, fill it, for Pete's sake*! So, on the surface, reading groups read books, but behind the scenes they do hundreds of other things that go largely unnoticed. However, both the invisible and the visible actions and benefits of associational life are woven together into a tapestry portraying local life. For this reason, the resident-connector team identified a series of typical associational activities that contribute to community well-being. They then asked each group which of these associational functions their group was performing and whether the group would be willing to perform new functions if asked.

In the table that follows, the left-hand column, marked "Activity," lists the many associational functions that contribute to the well-being of any town and its residents. The second column from the left, marked "Already Involved," shows that the sixty-two groups perform 299 functions that contribute to the town's productive capacity and well-being. After seeing the inventory of these 299 functions, one member of the resident research team said that he was very surprised to see how many community functions were performed that had previously been invisible to him. When they became visible to him, he said, "I didn't realize what the associations were doing. Now I can see that if these associations stopped functioning, the town would fall apart. It would die."

The third and fourth columns, marked "Not involved, Willing" and "Probably Willing," indicate the community functions that the groups were not doing but would do or probably would do if they were asked. These responses indicate that the town's associations are or probably are prepared to take on 285 additional community functions if asked. This pool of unused capacities is a tremendous new force waiting to be invited to contribute to the local well-being of every neighborhood and town.

So, what does this mean for a neighborhood like yours? In every neighborhood there is powerful unused potential for creative work, problem-solving, and the creation of a culture of contribution. This potential will become visible when neighbors' capacities become known and are connected individually and collectively, and when neighborhood associations are invited to contribute even more to the good of the community.

Residents who become active in issuing the invitation are sometimes limited by fear of rejection. Nonetheless, as the research described in this chapter (and elsewhere) demonstrates, both neighbors and their associations are waiting and willing to contribute their capacities to the well-being of their neighborhood or town.

Associational Functions Performed by Sixty-Two Local Associations

Activity	Already Involved	Not Involved, Willing	Probably Willing	Probably Not	Uncertain
Welcome Newcomer	15	21	7	17	1
Neighborhood Beautification	14	8	25	0	3 slight, 1 possibility
Parks and Recreation	14	12	7	22	1 possibility
Youth	34	4	8	14	0
Disabilities	22	16	6	17	0
Seniors	30	10	4	11	1 consider it
Homeless/ Hungry	24	8	6	18	2
Natural Disasters	18	12	6	21	1
Arts and Culture	34	4	1	13	5
Families	30	8	3	18	0
Health, Physical and Mental	28	7	4	20	1 maybe
ESL	0	6	6	47	1, 1 maybe
Family/Child Abuse	7	12	6	33	2, 1 maybe
Youth at Risk	12	10	4	30	2
Environment	17	10	5	23	2
History and Heritage	17	14	6	18	1 might
Recruit Teenagers	15	13	6	16	0

Key to the Good Life #5: Once we actually figure out what we want in order to have a Good Life, we realize that to get it we have to engage in gift exchange. Here's the rub: a gift is not a gift until it's given and received. Sometimes fear of rejection stops us from asking for what we want or offering our gifts to others, for fear we are not good enough. The good news is that our neighbors are happy to contribute and to receive gifts, but there's a catch: they are waiting to be asked. So, the Good Life cannot be achieved without an element of positive risk. It requires a level of faith on our part, that our neighbors will be there to receive us.

· · ·

So far, in this section of the book we have examined how connectors connect the hidden treasures of a neighborhood. We've done so, first, in order to show how to increase neighborly connections for their own sake, because those connections matter deeply in their own right, regardless of what they outwardly produce; and second, to show how to intentionally enhance the capacities of our neighborhoods to produce the irreplaceable elements that support our health, wealth, and power in ways that, through collective "neighbor power," only they can. In the next and final chapter of this part of the book, we shift from asking *how* to asking *what*. What is the unique work of people deeply connected, individually as well as collectively in neighborhoods? We know that the function of a hospital is to patch us up when we're sick. The hoped-for functions of schools are also self-evident, but what are the functions of a Connected Neighborhood?

CHAPTER 6

The Seven Functions of Connected Communities

The cynic might argue that in modern industrialized societies our sole purpose is to individually consume our share of the commonwealth by purchasing goods and services from the marketplace, or advocate that institutions assume the lion's share of the responsibility for the provision of health, safety, child-raising, economic and ecological stewardship, care, and production of food that appeals to diverse personal preferences regardless of environmental impact.

We believe that this outlook is hazardous to all our futures and the future of our planet. So, as an alternative, we affirm that our shared purpose as neighbors is to produce the common good by assuming principal functions in the areas of health, safety, raising our children, economic and ecological stewardship, care, and local (carbon neutral) production of nutritious food, and in this way to make practical the slogan, "Think global, act local."

So far, we have considered how best to discover and connect what is local, but the question remains, *What are we inviting our neighbors to do together?* Or put another way: *Aside from connecting for neighborliness, what other functions do vibrant neighborhoods undertake?* In answer to this question, we'd like to nominated the following seven irreplaceable community functions:

1. Enabling health
2. Ensuring security
3. Stewarding ecology
4. Shaping local economies
5. Contributing to local food production
6. Raising our children
7. Co-creating care

From Blue Ribbons to Community Functions

After the violent murder of her brother in 1955, the famous Italian artist Maria Lai vowed never to return to the village of her birth, Ulassai in Sardinia, Italy. That pledge was to be tested in 1979, when the Mayor of Ulassai tried to commission her to create a memorial for those who had died during World War I. Initially she refused, famously telling him that if he wanted to do something that would be meaningful to locals, he ought to commission something for the living that involved them, not a monument to the dead that ignores the living. She eventually gave in and accepted the commission, but not to create a war monument. She agreed that she would work with locals to create a piece of performance art that would make visible the invisible social and emotional ties that bound them together. No one could have imagined the outcomes that ultimately unfolded. Not alone did she and the locals reweave their deeply fragmented and traumatized village; they laid the foundations for a socially functioning and economically vibrant community that has been going from strength to strength over the last four decades.

The Story of the Blue Ribbon

In conversations with villagers between 1979 and 1981, Maria noticed that a piece of folklore kept being featured. The story was about a young girl who one day went to bring food to local shepherds on the mountain. When a sudden storm blew in the shepherds took cover in a nearby cave.

The girl, however, did not follow them. To their alarm, she ran off into the storm instead. Apparently, so the story goes, she followed a beautiful blue ribbon right into the eye of the storm and eventually caught it as the storm subsided. Jubilant, she returned to the cave to show the ribbon to the shepherds. But when she arrived, the entrance to the cave was blocked; there had been a landside, which had claimed the lives of all the men.

Maria recognized the significance of the story and that, whether fact or fiction, it held deep meaning for the locals. Ulassai had been troubled by serious conflicts between neighbors for years, but the people living there all individually held hopes of moving toward an alternative future with less conflict and more collaboration. The spontaneous action of a little girl, in her pursuit of beauty and vision, ultimately saved her life and was a powerful symbol of what those living in Ulassai were secretly yearning for.

Maria's performance art suggestion, inspired by the story of the little girl, was to bind together all of the houses of the thousand-plus villagers with one continuous and very long sky-blue denim ribbon and then to tie the houses to the mountain, revealing all of the relationships in the village and visibly celebrating the ties that bind. But the local conflicts ran so deep that there was an immediate negative reaction to her suggestion.

Just when it seemed that all was lost, a group of local women who were supportive of the idea went to each person who had concerns and talked those concerns through. The people who were resistant had valid concerns; they were against the idea because they wanted something that honestly reflected their real community. So this small group of connectors agreed on a compromise: they would use a code to authentically portray the kinds of relationships that existed in the village. The ribbon's message, or code, worked as follows:

- Where there was conflict between neighbors, the ribbon would be straight and stretched at the corner, using the sharp edges of their houses to symbolize the strain in their relationship.

- Where relations were neighborly, there was a knot.

- A bow represented friendship.

- A traditional festive loaf of bread was tied in the ribbon where people in different houses had married or fallen in love.

This powerful community-building initiative was documented through photography and video for future generations. Something magical and enduring happened the day they hung the ribbons. Basic relational foundations for collective change were made visible in a genuine way. More than forty years later, building on these foundations, this remote village is thriving. Among other things, it has a world-renowned cooperative textile industry. Its tourist trade is a major source of local income, and the village is especially attractive to mountaineers, bikers, and trekkers. As well as enhancing the local economy, the blue ribbon that was woven through the village in 1981 (or at least the process that brought it about) created a supportive net that has enabled villagers to reduce the level of conflict and violent crime in Ulaasai, ensuring a greater sense of security there.

Residents are also significantly healthier today than they were prior to this initiative, with many locals living past one hundred years old, and remaining active and well. The fabric of the built and natural environments has all the hallmarks of a place that enjoys significant local investment and stewardship. Equally striking is how many young people grow up and remain in the village, or return to raise families of their own there. And they can expect to eat well and age well in this beautiful part of the world, because the cooperative ethos does not stop with crafts and textiles. Local co-ops are also producing stunning artisan foods while others are coming up with some very innovative ways that people with extra needs for care and support can receive those within their own homes and remain interdependent with village life. In effect, after some forty years they continue to assume the seven functions of a Connected Community.

The Seven Foundational Functions

How might we describe each of the seven foundational community functions?

Enabling Health

Our neighborhoods and other small local places are, when transformed into communities, the primary source of our health. How long we live and how often we are sick are largely determined by our personal behaviors, social relationships, physical environment, and income. As neighbors, we are the people who can change these things for one another. Medical systems and doctors cannot change these factors, only we can—through collective effort. Most informed medical leaders advocate nonmedical community health initiatives, because they recognize that their medical systems have reached the limits of their health-giving power.

Health, properly understood, has very little to do with medicine. It is more about community and social justice than medicine. In fact, the scientific evidence tells us that 85 percent of what determines our health and well-being is related to community and economic connections; only 15 percent relates to medicine.[1] Recent studies by Julianne Holt Lunstad, a senior academic researcher at Brigham Young University, prove that the most powerful tool available for healing human suffering is community connections. All other tools, professional and technological, merely supplement this.

The jury is in, and the bad news is that disconnected communities are very harmful to our health. The good news is that the solution is in our hands and those of our neighbors. So powerful is the potential of such caring local connections that if you are someone who has no associational connections and tomorrow you join a local group, you will (statistically) reduce your chance of dying next year, by 50 percent.[2] When it comes to your health and the health of your loved ones, there is no known drug that can offer you better odds than your community can.

Consider the impact of the neighborhood ice rink in North Glenora, Edmonton, in Alberta, Canada. In Edmonton it typically starts to snow in late November or early December. To create an ice pond for a rink, the air needs to be cold enough for the water to freeze but not so cold that it freezes too quickly and ends up bumpy and uneven. It is quite a delicate art. Currently, thirteen community members, three of whom are kids, make up the volunteer rink-building team. There has been a rink in North Glenora since the community was founded in 1953. The rink was built before most of the houses and well before any other amenities, including the school. The rink has always been a community undertaking. Don Eastcott, a resident in his nineties has been there from the beginning. He says, "The rink was built by community spirit." He recalls how, in the early 1950s, community members would sign up for shifts around the clock (literally 24 hours a day) until it was complete. They would first stamp down the snow with their boots or snowshoes, then use a garden hose to flood the surface.

The rink is available for any individual to use. It is also used by the community's pond hockey team. This rink differs from the rinks used by typical hockey teams in the city: it is much cheaper, hyper-local, run by volunteers, noncompetitive, multiage, and multigender. The North Glenora hockey team is therefore much more inclusive than most sports teams. Without a doubt this ice rink is a *health enabler,* precipitating both physical health and mental health as folks get outside in the winter and enjoy social connectedness, fun, laughter, and cooperation. Plus, they create and maintain it!

Ensuring Security

Whether we are safe and secure in our neighborhood is largely within our domain. Many studies show that there are two major determinants of local safety: (1) how many neighbors we know by name, and (2) how often we are present and associated in public—that is, outside our houses.[3] Police activity, even when it is community centered, is still only a secondary protection compared to these two community actions. Therefore, most informed police leaders advocate for community alternatives to heavy-handed enforcement and surveillance.

As a sidebar to the North Glenora experience with their rink, Don Eastcott remembers a period in the 1970s when the rink was suffering frequent vandalism. Upon speaking with the local youth, adult volunteers found out that a boy named John was the culprit. A community member decided to repair and rebuild parts of the rink that had fallen into disrepair. He reached out to John and asked him to be his "foreman." The adults created a crew of young people who together rebuilt the perimeter of the rink. The kids, and especially John, became the stewards of the rink and really took ownership of it. This process also led to several youth becoming members of the neighborhood's Community League, a volunteer, not-for-profit association formed to meet the needs and interests of residents. Community leagues are recognized by the City of Edmonton as the primary speaking body for neighborhoods. The point here is that when you do community work, you don't stay stuck in any one function; you move around, creating safety, health, love, and care, all mixed together.

The city of Milwaukee, Minnesota, in the United States has developed the Blueprint for Peace,[4] a community-driven response to the complex factors that drive violence in the city. Rooted in public health and community-centered approaches to violence prevention and safety promotion, the Blueprint pushes resources and authority upstream into the hands of the communities most impacted by violence, racial inequity, and structural racism. By hiring local organizers, they are reconnecting these neighborhoods and, given that standard police practices have largely failed and sometimes profoundly harmed communities of color, supporting them in creating community-driven alternatives to police responses. This initiative stands out due to its proposals around restorative justice, alternative sentencing, and changing policing practices, in terms of stop-and-search and arrest protocols, all of which have done a lot to inflame violence rather than keep the peace. Guns, drugs, and mental health challenges consistently undercut some very good community-building efforts, so the fundamental test for the Blueprint for Peace strategy is in how well they can proactively address these issues rather than merely respond to some incident or crime.

Stewarding Ecology

The future of the Earth calls on us to "think global, act local." The "energy problem" is our local domain because how we transport ourselves, how we heat and light our homes, and how much waste we create are major factors in saving our earth.

Take climate change, for example. Most of the energy we use to light our communities, run our cars, heat our homes, and power our local businesses comes from giant, distant, toxic, and nonrenewable sources of energy. The real alternative is for local communities to plan, finance, and produce their own local, renewable energy that is reliable, safe, and sustainable—and to do it in ways that can bring a net financial return to local economies.

The people living on the Scottish Isle of Eigg are beacons of what is possible when communities take on this function. As mentioned in chapter 1, they became energy sufficient in 2008, when they became the first placed-based community in the world to go completely off-grid. Today they rely solely on wind, water, and solar power.

In cities around the world, families living on low incomes are more and more hard-pressed to afford their utility costs. In the United States, a number of communities have moved to challenge monopoly electric utilities. For example, in Maine a citizen-led campaign is steadily advancing to convert the utility serving most of the state into a consumer-owned electric company, allowing for competition and innovation on the public grid. Using antitrust legislation, communities in a growing number of other states are organizing to push back against outside monopolies that are not making the necessary investment to upgrade policy and practice to produce a clean, carbon-free future. Indeed, some monopolies are not just neglecting their responsibilities to the environment and the communities from which they profit, but rather are blocking plans to enable customer-owned rooftop solar power. As the next chapter shows, sometimes you've got to organize some pushback (not only against monopolies) to gain the power to be locally productive.

Shaping Local Economies

In our villages and neighborhoods, we have the power to build a resilient economy that is less dependent on the mega systems of finance and production that have proven to be so unreliable. Many successful enterprises begin locally, in garages, basements, kitchens, and dining rooms. As neighbors, we have the local power to nurture and support these businesses so that they have a viable market. In doing so, we also have the local power to capture our own savings, through cooperative groups, credit unions, and land trusts. Importantly, these endeavors are also the most reliable sources of nearby jobs, for in many communities, word-of-mouth among neighbors is still the most important access to employment.

One of the more significant studies of what generates local wealth in a city economy was conducted by Gallup for the Knight Foundation.[5] (The John S. and James L. Knight Foundation is an American nonprofit foundation that provides grants in journalism, communities, and the arts.) *The Soul of Community*, a three-year study, sought to determine the factors that connect residents to their communities, and the role of community attachment in an area's economic growth and well-being. The study focused on the emotional side of the connection between residents and their communities, and on the relation between that community attachment and economic growth. It found that cities with the highest levels of attachment had the highest rate of GDP growth.

Contributing to Local Food Production

We see a growing realization that an important community competency is the production of the food we eat. We are allied with the local food movement, supporting local producers and markets. In this way, we are doing our part to solve the energy problem caused by transportation of foodstuffs from places and even continents far away. We are doing our part to make sure our currencies circulate locally and we are improving our health by eating food free of poisons and not reliant on petroleum. Backyards, community gardens, and locally owned farms are therefore primary sites for local economic renewal and environmental sustainability, as well as for producing nourishing food.

An important example comes from Singapore. "I Wish You Enough" was the profound yet simple message that residents from the South Central Community in Singapore settled on as a way of starting a fresh conversation about the most necessary of human staples: food.

The statement has a flip side for those who live with plenty or with excess: I Wish You Enough reminds us that enough is enough and excess can be shared. The message has been used as a call to action and to encourage a spirit of sharing—what is known in Singapore as *kampung spirit*, which refers to a strong sense of community whereby neighbors look out for one another.

The I Wish You Enough call to action has led to neighbors setting up public booths where they share meals prepared with other neighbors. They have also undertaken hundreds of one-on-one conversations, walking around and having "chitchats" and offering delicious and varied dishes. Through these conversations they have come up with multiple practical ways of improving food sovereignty, so that as much as possible the people who consume the food, not distant market institutions, also control its production and distribution. The I Wish You Enough movement has become a vivid demonstration of what happens when a neighborhood decides to collectively address the issues of food shortage and food waste: it aims to ensure that everyone has enough.

Working against the dominant culture of possessive individualism and consumerism, neighbors in South Central Singapore are sharing time and food with one another, not as an act of charity but as an act of solidarity and neighborliness. I Wish You Enough is an anchor statement that underscores the trend toward food sovereignty everywhere, not just in Singapore. It's about taking back control of what goes into our bodies and exploring fun ways to produce local nutritious foods, redistribute food that's now going to waste, and repatriate food that is going to landfills. That's not so easy in neighborhoods with few close and affordable places to buy decent food.

Raising Our Children

We are all local people who must raise our children. We all like to say that it takes a village to raise a child, yet in modernized societies this is rarely true. Instead we pay professionals employed by institutional systems—teachers, counselors, coaches, youth workers, nutritionists, doctors, McDonalds, and social media—to raise our children. As families, we are often reduced to being responsible for paying others to raise our children and for transporting them to their paid child-raisers. Many of our villages have become incompetent at child-raising, seldom being responsible for our children or our neighbors' young ones. As a result, we talk about the local "youth problem" everywhere. There is no "youth problem." There is a village problem; adults have forgone their responsibility and capacity to join their neighbors in sharing knowledge and experience with their children and in receiving their children's wisdom in return.

At Southwood High School in Shreveport, Louisiana, forty local dads stepped up after three days of serious brawling in the school that led to twenty-three pupil arrests. They set up Dads on Duty. Each day a healthy number of them show up in the halls and "love their children to peace." With dad jokes and high fives, these papa bears have ended violence, almost overnight. The tender and solid presence of father figures who care has restored equilibrium. They did what the very best principals, teachers, school counselors, and police could not do effectively, no matter how hard they tried. They wrapped a halo of village-like support around those kids. The message was as simple as it was clear: "We're here, we love you, you're safe." The elders of the village showed up, not because they were paid but because they cared, and the kids calmed down.

Co-creating Care

Hospitable communities are the best site of local care. Our institutions can only offer service, not care. We cannot purchase care. Care is the freely given commitment from the heart of one to another. As neighbors, we care for one another. We care for our children. We care for our elders. And it is this care that is the basic power of a community of citizens. Care cannot be provided, managed, or purchased from systems. Our neighborhood future is made possible by our power to care. So, it is the new connections and relationships we create locally that further build community, because in joining together with one another, we manifest our care for the children, our neighbors, the earth, and our democracy, which flourishes when we care for our freedom and responsibility.

Consider Pat Worth's experience of "care" (see Foreword). Pat (1955–2004) was a cofounder (along with multiple others, including Richard Ruston, Catherine Fortier, Peter Park, Paul Young, John Cox, and Gordon

Fletcher, to name just a few) of the People First movement, which started in Canada. He lived in Toronto, Ontario, and was classified/labeled "mentally retarded" when he was a child in the mid-1950s. He was put into an institution. One day, when he was about sixteen, he fled the place. Later in his life he told John McKnight about his experience of living homeless on the streets of Toronto. "I lived on a park bench, where other people from Toronto slept." He said it was home. Gradually he met more people and, "through chance and good fortune," began to build a new life.

Along the way, Pat came to the conclusion that he wanted to be an organizer of people who were like him, who had experienced being labeled and pushed into "helping" institutions but had somehow gotten away, escaped, like he did. He wanted to organize them to collectivize their power for themselves and for those who have not yet gotten away but want to. So he conceived of an organization that came to be known as People First, a model that is now operating in many parts of the world. Pat was the person who began it in earnest, and for him, "People First means we're not 'retarded' people. We're people first; stop labeling us."

The People First movement began in Canada in 1973, when self-advocates with intellectual disabilities joined forces to assert their human rights. Their first issue was their right to live in the community—to get out of institutions—and have their voice, their choice, and their rights. Throughout the rest of the 1970s, People First groups formed all over Canada.

By the mid-1980s, they were a force to be reckoned with; they had organized a national platform called the Self Advocacy Development Project. By the late 1980s, the official People First of Canada organization began. It was incorporated on April 6, 1991.

Since that time, People First has evolved as a movement and as a national organization. It continues to grow, advancing on many of its issues and priorities and watching Canada, in large part due to the efforts of People First, become a leader in inclusion. Its work on human rights continues, and today the People First movement is at the forefront of changing society on issues of deinstitutionalization, equal employment, inclusive education, citizenship, inclusion, and meaningful community participation.

Author John McKnight warmly recall's traveling across Canada with Pat in the early days of the movement, organizing local People First groups with those whose experiences were similar to Pat's. One of the things Pat said when their trip was done made a significant impression on John: "Now John, you see, we are called disabled. But we are not disabled. We are *dis* but not disabled. We're *dis*connected." He concluded, "What we have been doing on this road trip is doing away with disability by substituting it with meaningful connections. And that's what we need. We don't need services; we need community."

Pat's wisdom in relation to the inclusion of people whose labels have made their gifts invisible and made them subject to the bigotry of the low expectations of others extends to other parts of modern life. In many neighborhoods, we don't just *dis* people with labels like "intellectually disabled." We *dis* people who don't fit our versions of "normal" in terms of mental health, gender, age, color, faith, and political outlook, to name just a few. These are ways we create walls of separateness and grow disconnected communities—what we term the "careless society." What Pat and People First advocate for is care that is freely given outside of managed spaces like institutions. The struggle continues.

The Interconnectedness of the Seven Functions

Even though we have discussed the seven neighborhood functions separately here, the truth is, they are interdependent. The connections between some functions are plainer to see than the connections between others. Nutritious local food plainly connects with health, the local environment, and local economies. Less obvious are the relationships between local food production and raising children, care, and safety; but on closer inspection the links are there, powerfully but invisibly so.

An Example from the West Side of Chicago: Where Many Functions Manifest

On the West Side of Chicago, thousands of two- and three-story buildings have flat roofs. In one neighborhood that has such buildings, they decided to build simple greenhouses on the top of low-rise flats.

These simple greenhouses hand-built of wood and plexiglass sheets have had many outputs over the years:

1. They have captured the heat escaping from the roof and used it to warm the greenhouses (stewarding ecology).

2. They have captured the heat and held it on the rooftops, so the greenhouses reduced the necessity for more heat in the buildings, thus reducing energy costs (shaping local economies, stewarding ecology).

3. They have captured the sunlight, thus adding to the seasonal growing capacity (stewarding local ecology, contributing to local food production).

4. They have produced nourishing food (contributing to local food production).

5. They have produced income from the sale of surplus food (shaping local economies).

6. Older local residents, many of whom had been raised in rural areas in the South, began to come to the greenhouse and grow food. This activity often revived them physically, mentally, economically, and spiritually, enabling them to live more healthful lives (enabling health, co-creating care).

7. A local school began to bring young students to learn about agriculture and energy conservation (raising our children).

8. These visits provided a hospitable and welcoming venue where young people could connect with productive adults in their neighborhood (raising our children, co-creating care).

9. The greenhouses created a sense of safety as neighbors literally watched over not just food but also one another; a lot can be seen from a rooftop greenhouse, and people can see the community activity taking place on the roof too (ensuring security).

In these ways, something that on the face of it was just about food also produced energy savings, income from sales, health for seniors, and education and care for students. The level of activity also created passive oversight that made the blocks safer.

Neighborhood life often involves very modest inputs—like the greenhouses—that appear, on the surface, to be one-dimensional; but when we look beneath the surface, we see that these seemingly simple inputs create multiple and diverse outputs with very little waste in between—the essence of productivity.

Key to the Good Life #6: Nothing lasts for long without a purpose. So, what is a neighborhood for? What is its purpose? The purpose of a neighborhood is to create a context and the essentials for a Good Life to be had by all who live there. For that purpose to come into everyday reality, neighbors have to take on some functions that only neighbors and their associations can perform. There are no external substitutes for this work. Community is a verb, not a noun. We must act our way thoughtfully and collectively toward it. It is through such collective action that we discover our community powers.

● ● ●

The seven functions offer different entry points to a vibrant neighborhood. Each of these entry points will attract different people, creating significant diversity among participants. Yet each participant will inevitably benefit from the collective efforts of their neighbors. The whole truly is greater than the sum of its parts.

Part Two of this book has focused on Connection. Drawing on Maria Lai's favorite medium for creating her art—the loom—for inspiration, we can sum up this chapter, and indeed the whole up to this point, as follows:

Each neighborhood is like a loom: the seven functions are the threads and the interconnections between these functions create a tapestry that reveals the health, wealth, and power of the Connected Community. In the chapters that follow in Part Three, we explore how best in practice to mobilize our community assets to fulfill their potential.

Three Tools for Connection

Tool 1: Finding Connectors

Try getting together with three neighbors to chat about the hallmarks of neighborhood connectors, which are as follows:

- *Connectors are gift-minded.* Like bees to a flower, resident connectors instantly know of a child who wants to learn to play a musical instrument when they hear of a local violinist.

- *Connectors are trusted by their neighbors.* Neighbors know that connectors are trying to join the dots in community and are not in it for themselves.

- *Connectors believe that their neighbors want to contribute to the well-being of the wider neighborhood, and that what they need is an invitation.* As a result, connectors are happy to make offers and extend invitations that their neighbors can't refuse.

- *Connectors feel welcome to get involved in other people's "business" and to invite others into public (shared) effort, or what some call "the commons."* They do so in a way that feels nonintrusive.

Once you and your three neighbors identify four other neighbors who you all agree are connectors, each of you make contact with one connector and have a similar conversation with them. It's a good idea to tell them why you see and value them as a connector, and to show them the list of hallmarks of connectors. Once you've gotten to know each other, ask them if they know three other neighbors who have the hallmarks of connectors. If the energy is there, take the next step and suggest that both of you go visit those neighbors, and so on. This creates a multiplier effect: starting alone, you enlarge your circle to four, then that group of four grows to eight, and eight grows to twenty. The beauty of this exercise is that it is pretty effortless, and there is no cold calling. It works on the principle that it often takes a connector to know a connector.

Tool 2: Listening Campaign/Learning Conversations

Once you've found a circle of connectors, try doing some listening in the neighborhood to discover what neighbors care about enough to take action on. This endeavor should not feel like hardship duty; instead, it should feel safe, doable, and manageable with the rest of life's challenges. You could start with the suggestion that each connector simply try having five learning conversations with neighbors on their block or street each week, then meet for coffee once weekly to share what is surfacing.

Here are some questions others have used to get a learning conversation going; They are not prescribed; change them around so they make sense to you.

- What do you care about enough to act on where you live?
- What local resources can you tap into to get going?
- Who else can you invite to join in?

The idea behind a listening campaign is that over the course of a few months, all of these one-to-one listening conversations will unearth a huge amount of energy, which in turn can be connected. As connectors hear about the gifts their neighbors would like to offer, they will also hear what people want. Matchmaking between neighborhood *offers* and *wants*—for example, by matching a neighbor who is happy to adopt another neighbor's potted plants while they are on vacation with a neighbor who wants that support is a very practical way to connect your street. More and more connectors are using digital assets and platforms, such as WhatsApp, or neighborhood-specific apps, such as Nextdoor, but there is no substitute for face-to-face learning conversations.

As you meet with other connectors each week, you will notice some common themes emerging across the various streets in the neighborhood. As that happens, and as you notice growing numbers of people and associations acting positively and investing their time and energy to generate solutions on their block or street, it might be time to bring together neighbors from different parts of the neighborhood. Consider organizing something like an ideas fair.

Tool 3: Ideas Fairs

An Ideas Fair is just a big party. It is not a meeting!

Connectors agree on a date and a venue. The basic ingredients are food, fun, and stories. The roles of the connectors are as follows:

1. *Invite (using personal one-to-one invitations) and convene the party.* To ensure that you include as many neighbors as possible, make sure that your inviting circle of connectors represents the diversity of your neighborhood. Be sure to invite folks from all walks of life and of all ages. The principle of personally welcoming the stranger is key.

2. *Host the party.* Hosting is about making sure neighbors have meaningful fun. The food and the entertainment can be sourced locally to showcase local talent, and the meaningful part is the quality and safety of the conversations that neighbors have. If you can, set up the room with small circular tables and seat no more than five people per table, so that they can get to know one another and feel safe.

Try encouraging people to share stories about times when their neighbors joined together to make things better. You could invite neighbors to bring along old photos or articles cut out of newspapers that capture what's strong about the neighborhood, as a way of getting conversations going at each table. After the food, entertainment, and storytelling are completed, ask people to discuss what would need to happen to create more of those positive neighborhood stories.

The Ideas Fair is also an opportunity for neighbors and associations to exchange practical ideas and forge alliances.

PART THREE

MOBILIZE

The focus of the third and final part of the book is on the *Mobilize* stage of community building. The third call to action is to *Mobilize*. We look at neighborhood mobilization under three distinct headings:

- **From Crisis to Connected.** Chapter 7 presents part 1 of a detailed practical guide for mobilizing community assets at the early stages of community building, starting with first encounters with connectors and associations at the neighborhood level, then moving toward a greater level of connectedness and early organizing.

- **From Envisioning to Collective Action.** Chapter 8 builds on part 1 of the practical guide for mobilizing community assets, going deeper into the practicalities of moving from one-to-one conversations and community gatherings to more focused community work and organizing for local impact.

- **The Role of the Useful Outsider.** In chapter 9 we explore some affirmative ways of moving from distrust or unhealthy dependence to mutual intent and useful alliances.

Mobilize at a Glance

	The Disconnected Neighborhood	The Connected Community	Keys to the Good Life
	Definition: Prioritizes relationships outside the neighborhood that separate neighbors from one another, and promotes individual survival over community well-being.	**Definition:** Nurtures neighborhood relationships that enable people to work together to create a Good Life.	**Definition:** Key lessons learned from neighborhoods on their journey toward deeper connection.
M O B I L I Z E	Chapter 7 is about the practical methods we can use to mobilize community power from crisis to connections.		
	Disconnected **Methods:** Leaders, planning, deficit/needs mapping, advocating for reform.	*Connected* **Methods:** Circle of connectors, learning conversations, asset mapping.	Key #7: Don't wait for a flood; instead, initiate a listening campaign in your neighborhood; give your neighbors a good listening to.
	Chapter 8 is about the practical methods we can use to mobilize community power from envisioning to collective action.		
	Disconnected **Methods:** Leaders, planning, deficit/needs mapping, advocating for reform.	*Connected* **Methods:** Community building, dialogue, parties/celebrations/hosting.	Key #8: The Good Life is made up of individual and associational gifts that are like shards of different-colored glass that form a mosaic. That mosaic is the context in which our personal stories and those of our neighbors and place combine.

Mobilize at a Glance, *continued*		
The Disconnected Neighborhood	The Connected Community	Keys to the Good Life
Chapter 9 is about shifting neighborhood relationships with outside actors away from wholesale distrust or unhealthy dependence and toward points of mutual intent that will result in useful alliances with Useful Outsiders.		
Disconnected **Orientation:** Seeks to recruit clients to their services/programs. Views neighborhoods as units of consumption.	*Connected* **Orientation:** Seeks to be useful to community life; cheers on community alternatives and features community capacities. Sees neighborhoods as creative and productive places.	**Key** #9: Preserve community authority to change the things that only you and your neighbors can change, and make useful alliances with reliable outsiders who understand how to relocate authority and provide support without directing the outcomes.

MOBILIZE

CHAPTER 7

Diary of a Neighborhood Made Visible and Vibrant

Part 1: Step by Step from Crisis to Connected

There is no paint-by-numbers way of making what is invisible in a neighborhood visible and vibrant. This said, there are some guiding principles and community-powered tools that open a space where relationships are leveraged, local solutions have value, the stranger is welcomed, and the Connected Community emerges. Believing that "the proof of the pudding is in the eating," this chapter seeks to season palates by telling the story of a place we call *Giftville*—a composite tale that brings together narratives from various places around the world, from neighborhoods we have had the privilege of learning both with and from.

We begin by sharing a quote that sums up our feelings about the ideas and tools we are about to share. It's found on the back cover of a 1973 cookbook called *Tassajara Cooking*:

> This is a book to help you actually cook—a cooking book. The recipes are not for you to follow, they are for you to create, invent, and test. It explains things you need to know, and things to watch out for. There are plenty of things left for you to discover, learn, and stumble upon. Blessings. You're on your own. Together with everything.

With this blessing and caution, we present a loose framework that the residents of Giftville came to recognize as they reflected on their journey years later. It is a path they happened upon and blazed through with passion and some frustration. They were searching for answers, possibilities, and connections, not a plan. In the end, they were guided by their instincts, their trust in one another, and their commitment to their neighborhood.

Giftville Framework: Creating the Connected Community

1. Stop, look, listen!
2. Discover the local resources:
   a. Find the connectors.
   b. Uncover the associations and networks.
   c. Unearth the gifts of head, heart, hands, and conscience.
3. Connect people and passions.
4. Identify outside resources to match neighbors' investments.
5. Find and use peace-building practices.
6. Appreciate what's great, and unlock what might be possible.
   a. What can we do with local people power?
   b. What can we do with help from outside agencies?
   c. What do we need outside agencies to do?
7. Gather and celebrate!
8. Assume a posture, not a project.

1. Stop, Look, Listen!

Our story begins with Imani, her husband Jamar, and a newspaper article. One evening, Imani and Jamar were discussing an article from a local newspaper. It wasn't the first article ever written about their neighborhood, but it was the final straw. Like previous articles, this one reported on drug use, high crime rates, the "ravages of unemployment," and the growing levels of fear in the area. Giftville could just as easily have been called "Grantsville," because it had a long history of receiving city, state, federal, and foundation grants, which were in turn funneled to social service agencies that attempted to "fix" the community's problems. The people of Giftville had watched funded initiatives and campaigns come and go over the years, with very little sustained progress to show for it. Yes, Giftville's residents had their challenges, but they were more than just problems to be fixed.

After reading the article, Imani and Jamar went for a walk to clear their heads. At the park they connected with some of their neighbors, who too were incensed by the article. They were all tired of the negative, unfair press their neighborhood was receiving. They began to share what their community meant to them and all the good things they'd experienced over the years. In that moment, they, not the newspapers, controlled the narrative. This conversation made its way back to Imani and Jamar's home.

That night many years ago, seven neighbors hatched a response and committed to a different sort of campaign—a *listening campaign*. They decided to give their neighbors "a good listening to" by holding conversations not unlike the one they were having in that moment. For fun and for courage, this group called themselves "The Magnificent Seven." In these conversations, The Magnificent Seven would listen for the resources in, and resourcefulness of, their neighborhood. In short, they would look for what was strong, not for what was wrong.

2. Discover the Local Resources

The Magnificent Seven's listening campaign had three goals:

1. To find connectors in the community
2. To uncover the resourcefulness of associations and networks
3. To unearth the hidden gifts of their neighbors—gifts of the head, heart, hands, and conscience

a. Find the Connectors

At the time, there were approximately five thousand people living in Giftville. It was an area rich in cultural diversity. The Magnificent Seven recognized that, as a group, they themselves were diverse, but not diverse enough to gain the trust of the majority of their neighbors. They could not do it alone.

They spent the first year trying to grow trust among their neighbors. They adopted the practice of drinking black decaffeinated coffee, mainly because they were to have hundreds of one-on-one coffee conversations over the next twelve months. They'd often say, "Black decaf is how community grows." Another concept that emerged early on was the need to identify connectors, a project they referred to as *neighbor-up*.

To neighbor-up meant leveraging the connections their neighbors already had in order to expand the listening network. During their one-on-one visits in search of connectors, they would ask the following question: *Are there ten people you know who would be open to talking with us? And would you introduce us to them?* If the answer was yes, chances were the group had found themselves a connector.

By spending time in learning conversations and in the places where they gathered or casually bumped into their neighbors, they found nearly one hundred connectors. They discovered that one connector often knew as many as fifty or more of their neighbors. It was clear that even before The Magnificent Seven got going, each of these connectors had already linked together a circle of neighbors. These individuals were naturals; they had been born into the world with this skill. They had the ability to build relationships without fanfare, with modest actions that kept them off the radar.

b. Uncover Associations and Networks

The importance of seeking out and identifying connectors was a great and early discovery made by The Magnificent Seven. Through this revelation they came to understand that their neighborhood was already loosely organized, but the ties that bound them were thin, short, and hard to see. At first, connectors tended to know only a few others of "their kind" on their block or through their associational networks, but not beyond that. The Magnificent Seven then began to explore the benefits of linking the connectors to one another.

Today, connectors in Giftsville meet regularly with intention. Nurturing the relationships among connectors has allowed neighborly circles to overlap in all sorts of surprising and meaningful ways. Because of this connector network, the community has the ability to influence the lives of every family and individual in Giftville, including those who were previously at the edge of neighborhood life. This didn't just happen; it took a lot of hard work, patience, and courage.

On one occasion, at a connectors meeting, Imani shared about a person she had met named Bob. Bob was in his late seventies and a skilled woodcarver who had a knack for carving walking sticks. In fact, he had about forty of them in his garden shed. When Imani first encountered him, Bob spoke of feeling lonely and having a deep sense of uselessness. Andrew, another connector at the meeting, knew what to do, or more accurately, he knew someone who knew someone who knew what to do. He knew a man named Muhammad who was a member of a seniors group in the area. Muhammad was also connected to a lot of craftspeople and carpenters. Andrew connected Imani to Muhammad, and Imani in turn introduced Muhammad to Bob. Through this connection and through connecting with the seniors group and other craftspeople, Bob was plugged back into the life of the neighborhood. Word of Bob's gift started to spread, and to this day he enjoys a very steady demand for his hand-carved walking sticks, which he shares at no cost to his neighbors. Bob also mentors young people in the neighborhood, teaching them the fading craft of whittling—the art of carving shapes out of wood with a knife. Some of the pieces created by Bob and his apprentices are on display at the local library.

c. Unearth the Gifts of Head, Heart, Hands, and Conscience

The one-on-one conversation was the cornerstone of The Magnificent Seven's work. The conversations they had were well planned, purposeful, and filled with the kinds of questions they felt would be impactful and useful locally. When speaking with her neighbors, Imani discovered that they had an abundance of gifts that were lying fallow, ungiven and unreceived. It is said that a gift is not a gift until it is given; it is also true that a gift is not fully expressed until it is received. In supporting her neighbors to discover their own gifts and the gifts of others, Imani found it helpful to categorize what she was hearing as gifts of the head, gifts of the heart, gifts of the hands, and gifts of conscience.

Gifts of the Head. These are things that neighbors know, such as knowledge about local history or local flora and fauna. Other neighbors are strong on reflection and discernment, having the ability to weigh facts and diverse perspectives and reach wise judgements in a way that includes others. Then there are those who are more mindful or thoughtful. They probe for the facts and opinions of all comers. Their nature is to be curious and open-minded. Their community gift is wisdom.

Gifts of the Heart. These gifts are emotional traits that individual neighbors possess and share willingly, such as empathy and warmth, care for people at the margins, and natural affection for and feelings of kinship toward others. This gift domain includes people with relational know-how, who are good at peacemaking, healing, bridge-building, and understanding group dynamics and unspoken emotions. Gifts of the heart feature strongly among connectors. They often speak of "the feel of things," having "a sense of the situation," and "going at at a pace that allows trust to be built." They pay attention to ways of hosting and welcoming, including those who have been excluded.

Gifts of the Hands. These gifts are talents that individual neighbors are proficient enough in to teach or support a neighbor—for example, cooking, gardening, and playing a musical instrument. People with gifts in this domain are of a practical disposition and in touch with their surroundings—their hands are "in the soil." They often speak of the "handmade," "homemade," "homespun," and "earthy." They like things to be practical, concrete, plainspoken.

Gifts of Conscience. These gifts are principles of fairness and social justice. They are the ideals and values that a neighbor is prepared to stand up for and step out from the crowd to stand by, such as taking affirmative stances in relation to racial equity, gender equality, inclusion, and economic justice. Gifts in this domain are related to courage, integrity, solidarity, and commitment. The gifted one often speaks of "the principle of the matter," asking, "Is this fair to all sides?" The right to say no, to dissent, matters hugely to them, and they won't commit to a circle where they and other members are prevented from doing so. They have an eye for the power dynamics within the neighborhood and, most importantly, between outside actors and the neighborhood. They regularly ask, "How can we better welcome the stranger?"

d. Discover-Explore-Connect Questions

As well as discovering the gifts of the head, heart, hands, and conscience, each one-on-one conversation helped the connector and neighbor to do the following:

- *Discover* the things that enrich the resident's life in the neighborhood.
- *Explore* which passions could be developed into new options and contributions to community well-being.
- *Connect* a resident's gifts to other resources in the neighborhood in order to create a visible and vibrant community.

Folks in Giftville came to describe these one-on-one conversations as Good Life Conversations, because they surfaced what a Good Life in their neighborhood would look like and what would need to happen locally to get there.

Following are samples of the questions asked during the one-on-one Good Life Conversations:

Discover	Explore	Connect
What do you like doing that makes you forget time?	If you could start a business, what would it be?	Where do you think you could make a contribution?
What gives you the greatest joy or pleasure?	What are the three skills you would most like to learn?	If three other people shared your interest, would you be willing to meet up?
What are your passions?	What kind of job (paid or unpaid) might be associated with your passions?	Where do you think you could share one of your gifts?
What are your concerns for the neighborhood?	What would you like to teach others?	What clubs or groups exist in your community that share your passions?

Let's take a moment to look in more detail at The Magnificent Seven's initial efforts. What else can we learn?

They recognized others. The Magnificent Seven were connectors in their own right. Each person was well-connected to their neighborhood, and each had the ability to recognize connector qualities in others. These qualities were identified mainly through one-on-one conversations. A question they would ask within this context also functioned as a call to action: *Are there ten people you know who would be open to talking with us, and can you make the introduction?*

They created a rhythm. The Magnificent Seven created a rhythm in their neighborhood. They would linger at the gates after dropping their kids at school. They would walk their dogs when parks were at their busiest. They frequented well-known spaces where people gathered or casually bumped into one another while living their neighborly lives. They took time for conversation, searching for other connectors, ever seeking to extend the circles of participation. The more conversations they had, the more neighbors they met. These neighbors often knew of other local connectors who were already weaving their part of the community tapestry.

They practiced curiosity. The Magnificent Seven took a keen interest in others. When engaging with them, they did not seek to control the conversation, but through questions they held a space in which others could share the often-hidden pieces of themselves. They learned about people's skills, passions, interests, and connections to others. During multiple one-on-one conversations, the name of a connector would surface several times. The Magnificent Seven saw this name as a potential lead, and when a connector was mentioned they would ask to be introduced. "Sanji sounds like a great person and someone I would really like to speak with. Could you introduce me?"

They spoke in stories, not statistics. Giftville was a neighborhood that had once been defined by statistics. The education rate, crime rate, unemployment rate, and so on were numbers used to tell a story of a community in dire need and of a people who did not have the capacity to do for themselves. The Magnificent Seven wanted to tell a different story, one that was coauthored with their neighbors. In their one-on-one conversations, they invited their neighbors to tell stories about times they and their neighbors had joined together to make things better. Moved by these stories, The Magnificent Seven decided to host a storytelling event at the Community Center. They invited people to come and share their stories at the microphone or to submit them in writing. They called the event "Mending Fences" because through it they wanted to restore the fractured relationships in their community. Sanji had the gift of photography and he documented the night through his lens. Following the event, The Magnificent Seven took the photos and stories and gathered their neighbors together to create an art installation by hanging these items on a fence adjacent to the local park. The park was their place and this was their story.

They hosted. The Magnificent Seven opened their homes to fifteen of the one hundred connectors they had identified. They spent time sharing with these connectors how positively their neighbors were speaking about them and about the impact they were having. In these conversations they also wanted to learn about the connectors' relationships to associational life: Were they part of an association? Could they identify associations that were active in their neighborhood? (We'll come back to how they used this information a little later.) They then invited the fifteen connectors, along with the rest of the connectors, to a community party and asked them to extend the invitation to at least four other neighbors from their block or street who they believed had the interests of the neighborhood at heart and were prepared to roll up their sleeves and contribute to their community's well-being.

They were tenacious. The Magnificent Seven had more than a thousand one-on-one conversations in four months, which led to the discovery of nearly one hundred connectors. Each conversation lasted on average thirty to sixty minutes; some went way beyond that. They met in people's homes, in coffee shops, on park benches, and on front steps. They held space for individuals who typically didn't have the floor at public meetings. They diligently sought to reveal the treasures hidden behind the labels.

They identified gifts. In addition to finding connectors, The Magnificent Seven were also interested in understanding the gifts, skills, and knowledge of each person. In calling these gifts out of their neighbors, they were affirming their neighbors' self-worth and taking inventory of the basic resources that could be used in building a stronger and more connected Giftville.

Key to the Good Life #7: If floods and other natural disasters spur neighborhoods to connect and to dig deep in order to respond to their crises, does that mean we must wait for a disaster to strike before we start building more Connected Communities? Fortunately, the answer is no. There are positive alternatives to disasters that are just as effective at spurring us toward the Good Life together. So, don't wait for a flood or other disaster; instead, initiate a listening campaign in your neighborhood; give your neighbors a good listening to. Try collecting connections instead of stuff, and get to know your neighbors before you need them.

• • •

Transitioning to Deeper Impact Organizing

Part 2 of this diary is presented in the next chapter, where we look at how the residents of Giftville built on their efforts to identify and connect a circle of connectors and sought to better understand and connect local associations. We journey with them from envisioning to collective action.

CHAPTER 8

Diary of a Neighborhood Made Visible and Vibrant

*Part 2: Step by Step from Envisioning
to Collective Action*

3. Connect People and Passions

One resident ended her Good Life Conversation by asking the connector, "Where have you been all my life?"

One-on-one conversations assisted The Magnificent Seven in connecting residents to one another through common passions, and they had a way of helping that to happen. During those conversations they would ask questions such as the following:

- What is something you care enough about in relation to your neighborhood that you would take action on it?
- What are some personal gifts and resources you would be willing to bring to that effort?
- What resources in the neighborhood could you and your neighbors tap into?
- Who else would be willing to join you in this effort and what would it take to encourage their participation?
- If I come across others who share your passion or who I believe could contribute to your effort, would you be willing to connect with them?

Framing the conversations in this way supported the residents of Gift-ville in identifying the things they cared about enough to act on collectively. It was also a great way of getting down to what people's priorities were. During these conversations, neighbors could potentially name as many as five issues; two might be things they felt others ought to do, one could be something they had strong opinions about but no motivation to act on, and two could be things they really cared about and were willing to act on. It was the two things they cared about that The Magnificent Seven—and over time, all the connectors—learned to focus on. Many of the people on the receiving end of these conversations found them life enhancing and sometimes life changing.

As they continued to identify gifts and priorities, The Magnificent Seven decided to throw a community party in late January.

The Community Party

As they did with their one-on-one conversations, The Magnificent Seven put a lot of thought into the party and organized it with intention. Here's how they did it:

1. Each of the 100-plus connectors received a personal invitation to the party. In the invitation they were encouraged to invite four of their neighbors who lived on their street or on their block.

2. Although they were going to talk "community business," they were intent on having a party, not a meeting.

3. They thought deeply about how to be inclusive and identified potential barriers to participation, giving attention to the time and date of the party, location, accessibility, dietary considerations, and so on.

4. To create an intimate setting, the tables were small and round with five people at each, including a host connector.

5. They actively encouraged people to mix and mingle so they could broaden their circle of participation in a fun and relaxed way.

6. Their entertainment showcased local talent.

7. They had a clear purpose and a process they followed that supported the development of a shared vision and commitment to some practical steps to realize the vision.

It was a party like no other party Giftville had ever seen. More than five hundred residents attended, almost 10 percent of the area's population. They had some serious fun and genuinely enjoyed one another's company while developing motivation and focus for more collective resident-led action. Here's how they orchestrated the party:

- The Magnificent Seven invited seven other connectors to join them in hosting the party. These hosts were intentionally chosen to include those who represented the diversity of the entire neighborhood. As the invited connectors arrived with the four other neighbors each had invited, the hosts greeted each connector by their first name. They were then shown to their tables. A local band played relaxing music as people at the tables conversed.

- Each table was dressed with a tablecloth, flowers, and lots of materials such as pens, markers, and Post-its. They were also decorated with photos and press clippings that guests had been invited to bring. These items drew attention to the things they were most proud of in relation to their block or street and neighbors.

- Once everyone had been shown to their tables, members of the hosting circle went from table to table and personally thanked the connectors for all they were doing in the neighborhood. They didn't just speak in generalizations; these thank-yous were personalized, as in the following example:

   ### How to Lift Up a Neighbor

   The Magnificent Seven started by saying something like the following:

   Deepti, thanks for all you do. It's great that you and your neighbors are here to celebrate all your achievements, and those of all the neighbors at the other tables.

They then got specific by following an assigned order they had created. They spoke about what the guest had been doing, the impact it was having on others, and how, as a result, things in the neighborhood had gotten better. Drawing from the details of their one-on-one conversations, they said:

What You Did: Deepti, I want to say a particular thank-you for connecting those four young men with Mrs. Greynor to help her with her overgrown backyard.

The Impact It Had: You know that meant so much to Mrs. Greynor and to those boys. Sadly, as you know, Mrs. Greynor died a few months ago. But those boys were at her funeral and they were so sad. You remember when Mrs. Greynor's son thanked them during the eulogy and told them how much their visits and neighborliness had meant to his mother? Bless me but didn't one of them stand up in the church and say she meant the world to him? She had started teaching him how to read again after he dropped out of school. She encouraged him to believe in himself once again. It makes me well up just thinking about it. Deepti, that happened because of you. Mrs. Greynor would never have trusted those boys but for you. If they were trustworthy in your book, they were trustworthy in hers. I suspect one or two of those boys came pretty unwillingly to the hard work they ended up having to do in Mrs. Greynor's backyard, but you encouraged them and loved them into it. You started a backyard revolution right there!

As a Result, in Our Neighborhood: That's just one of the many, many connections you've helped form. You know what's interesting, Deepti? The ripples from your connecting are being felt throughout the neighborhood. When we spoke with folks on your block, they told us that, as a result of what happened between those boys and Mrs. Greynor, the connections between seniors and young people are better than ever. It has inspired others, young and old, to reconnect. We are becoming a community once again because of you, and this party is for you, to say thank-you to you and everyone like you in our neighborhood.

Without exception, every connector—somewhat embarrassed—responded to their host's affirmation by saying, "I didn't do anything special, just what you do as a neighbor, right?" But of course what they did was special and uncommon. In a world that lifts up leadership, this sort of connectorship can get missed. That night, The Magnificent Seven lifted up the connectors, with gratitude, to their rightful places as makers and producers. As a result, others at each table were themselves inspired to do more connecting and had great examples of how to do so.

Having thanked each of the connectors, The Magnificent Seven then asked them to introduce the Magnificent Seven to each of the neighbors at the table. They then asked the connector to scan the room to see if there was anyone there they didn't know. Once the connector spotted someone they didn't recognize, the host invited the connector to follow them to that person and made introductions. They then went back to the original table and asked the other neighbors if they could see anyone they didn't know yet and invited them to take a risk and go say hello. Soon after that, the room was buzzing with conversation and laughter. The ice was broken, the party had begun.

Shortly after, people were encouraged to take their seats and were invited to share stories from their block or street about a time when neighbors joined together to make things better. The photos and newspaper cuttings that adorned the tables were used to animate the conversation. After about twenty-five minutes of story sharing, while the connectors stayed at their assigned tables, the four neighbors each had brought were encouraged to go to four different tables to hear other stories and share their own stories with people from other parts of the neighborhood. This activity created an incredible number of ideas as people heard all the different initiatives that their neighbors were engaged in, and it created powerful reinforcement for these local efforts. As people's efforts were validated, they became more open to receiving new ideas.

It was then time for some food and more entertainment. Five jazz musicians provided some energizing music to the conversations that hummed around the community hall. People could move around and sit wherever they felt most comfortable.

After eating, it was time to "share some stories that inspired you from your conversations tonight." Microphones were passed around and people shared what had struck them, excited and motivated them. The stories they shared further reinforced local efforts and formed an oral tapestry of all that was strong within their neighborhood.

Next came an awards ceremony. Each one of the one hundred connectors was invited to the front of the hall to receive their "unsung heroes" award. It was one of the most moving experiences that most people in that hall had ever had. In that moment, they were a powerfully Connected Community, and together they were enough—a truly visible and vibrant neighborhood.

Once the awards ceremony was completed, desserts were served. As the dessert plates were removed, the hosts invited people to go back to their original tables if they weren't already there. Then they were asked to dream out loud with the neighbors on their block or street about what they wanted to see happen and what they were willing to contribute to their block or street and to the wider neighborhood. The connectors were asked to pay close attention to what themes emerged.

As the evening ended, the themes were gathered and written on flip-chart paper near the exit door. As people left to go home, they were invited to choose a theme that they wanted to take forward and work on. They were told where the group working on that theme would meet and their contact details were taken.

Festival of Ideas

Weeks after the party, The Magnificent Seven and the wider hosting circle convened a weekend event in which the groups that had formed around themes of interest met in different buildings and locations around Giftville. They called this gathering a *Festival of Ideas*. The Festival provided a platform for getting more practical and committing to some initiatives to address the themes that had emerged at the community party. They decided on some practical steps, then addressed the following questions:

1. What could they do together as neighbors to take the initiative forward?

2. What did they need in terms of outside help to support the initiative?

3. What was beyond their neighborhood power that required the help of outside actors?

The Community Walk

After starting the day with pancakes and practical ideas and possibilities, it was time to go for a community walk. As they toured the neighborhood, each theme group searched for primary resources they could tap into to move forward on their priorities. As they walked, participants were invited to think on, but were not limited to, the following questions:

- Where are the cared-for places?
- What public spaces are provided for children, teenagers, or adults?
- Where are the places with potential?
- Where do people sit, relax, or relate?
- Where are the places of life, hope, and beauty?
- Where do you feel a sense of connection?
- Where are the places that people gather?
- What spaces are available for community initiatives?
- Where do people like to meet?
- Where do people feel especially safe?

As the group walked through their neighborhood, it was as though they were walking through it for the first time, because this time they were viewing it through a lens of abundance, not scarcity. As a result, they were able to identify all sorts of built and natural assets.

So far in this process, the folks of Giftville had managed to do a wonderful job engaging the personal and physical resources of their neighborhood, but they didn't stop there. They knew that there were three basic entry points to creating the Connected Community and making the invisible visible: (1) the assets of individuals, (2) physical assets, and (3) associational assets. To identify the third entry point, the hosting circle created an inventory of associations.

Inventory of Associations

The hosting circle used a range of methods to inventory their neighborhood associations, including the following:

- Reviewing public sources such as newspapers, community notice boards, community directories, newsletters, bulletins, and so on
- Interviewing leaders of local formal associations
- Interviewing leaders of local religious congregations
- Interviewing connectors
- Interviewing residents and community activists
- Conducting random telephone surveys

When interviewing people from associations, some of the following questions were asked:

1. As an association, what do you do?
2. What do you do that helps people other than the members of your organization?
3. What are you willing to do that you are currently not doing?
4. How are you currently serving the community?
5. What are ways you have offered support to community initiatives?
6. How can your association become more community-serving?

Having identified many associations, the hosting circle sat with each of the themed groups and heard about their priorities and the individual and associational resources they planned to use. It was time to have more intentional conversations about the associations and how they could be useful to each initiative.

Grow Associational Life

In the early spring, The Magnificent Seven gathered with thirty-four neighborhood connectors from the themed groups who had deep relationships at the block level and/or with issues and affinity groups in the neighborhood. Their shared purpose was to map out all the local formal and informal associations that had been identified. They then agreed to a process for speaking to each association about what they were currently doing and what other activities they might be willing to engage in. They shared with the associational leaders the priorities that were emerging from the themed groups and explored how the associations might like to contribute.

By now the initiating group of seven had expanded and become a series of overlapping groups of connectors. Through the earlier process of one-to-one conversations, the community party, and themed action groups, they had gained a very strong sense of the various priorities that residents cared about enough to act on. With that knowledge and influence, they would share those priorities with representatives of the various associations to find out which priorities their members would like to support. They also asked how these associations could potentially collaborate in moving things forward.

4. Identify Outside Resources to Match Investments

The themed groups also worked on identifying some outside resources that would match the groups' investments in time and resources. They learned about grant opportunities, certification classes, and organizational leaders who were adept at clearing a way for community-driven efforts. In leveraging these resources, they were always cautious not to get pulled into the deficit map by identifying as passive recipients or needy or "deserving" clients.

5. Find and Use Peace-Building Practices

At this point, it is necessary to recognize that in community-building work, conflicts can arise. Giftville was not immune. Conflicts occurred at different levels and with different degrees of seriousness throughout the process. Some conflicts were deeply uncomfortable for The Magnificent Seven, but they faced them and found that conflict is not always a bad thing. It often provided an opportunity to clear the air, resulting in a renewed drive and sense of energy afterward.

There is no straightforward and easy way to resolve conflicts between neighbors, but The Magnificent Seven found some peace-building practices that they incorporated into their approach:

Peace-Building Practices Useful in Community Building

1. Find out what people disagree about. Let them present this information to each other in their own words. Remind people that it is OK to have doubts and to say no to certain things if they disagree. Remind people to object without being objectionable. Opinions are important but they are never more important than authentic community-building efforts.

2. Ask how the neighbors experiencing the conflict feel and how they think the conflict can be resolved or if they feel it needs to be resolved. Sometimes a little tension can be healthy.

3. Consider all the different suggestions for a solution, if they surface.

4. Consider what we can agree on and when we must agree to disagree.

5. Make sure that strong voices aren't dominating more careful, reflective, and quiet neighbors.

6. Give those involved tips and guidelines for how to live with one other despite disagreement. Disagree without being disagreeable.

7. Find peace-builders in the local community.

8. Share stories of nonviolent conflict, inclusion, and peace.

It is important to note that living side by side with people who think differently than one another is the sign of a confident and healthy community. Not everyone in the community-building process has to always agree. If your groups genuinely represent the diversity of the area, there will be a diversity of ideas and opinions. This diversity is a strength, not a problem. As Peter Block says, "If you can't say no, your yes is meaningless."[1]

6. Appreciate What's Great and Unlock What Might Be Possible

Just before summer, all the participating association and themed citizen action groups discovered a useful and sometimes quite significant way of supporting one another. There was a sense of shared confidence in the air, and a growing pride in the neighborhood. The people of Giftville were no longer the passive recipients of services. Together they determined the things they had the power to do for themselves, the initiatives that required outside support, and the issues that were better served by outside agencies and institutions. One of the priorities that came up time and time again was including the voices and contribution of young people.

The youth crime rate was the statistic of choice for local newspapers. They would speak of Giftville youth as problems to be fixed, not as gifts to be revealed. Fingers were pointed as people spoke of "those kids" and "that gang." The Magnificent Seven reminded their neighbors that "those kids" were "our kids" and "that gang" was part of "our gang." Neighbors determined that they wanted to work on pairing the young people in their community with caring and productive adults. What emerged came to be known as The Skills Library.

The Skills Library

After school, many of the neighborhood youth would gather outside the community center and slowly make their way into the lobby, where they would clown around, shout, and disrupt the other patrons. On more than one occasion, community center staff asked the youth to leave; in some instances the police were called. A retired high school teacher named Clyde attended the center and began taking an interest in the youth who gathered there. Clyde had participated in one of the action groups and was also a connector. In observing the youth, he noticed that many came to the center right after school and stayed until the center closed. These young people wouldn't go home for dinner; rather, they would buy junk food from the vending machine. Another observation was that every interaction an adult had with the youth served to discipline them. Finally, there wasn't a designated space in the center for the youth to hang out in.

One day, before school had finished for holidays, Clyde asked the community center staff if he could book the vacant room adjacent to the lobby and set out some tables and chairs. They agreed. Once the school bell rang and the youth poured into the lobby, Clyde approached them and introduced himself. He then asked, "Who's hungry?" The youth shouted in unison, "We are!" He then asked, "Do any of you know a great place to order pizza?" They all suggested the pizza joint up the street. Clyde then asked, "Who would like to come and help me get the pizza?" He thought one or two of them would volunteer; he was surprised when the whole group wanted to help. Clyde walked to get the pizza with twenty young people in tow. When they returned with their food, they sat around the tables that Clyde had set up. As they ate, he asked them about their day, their favorite subjects in school, and things they liked to do. At the end of the night, a couple of the youth asked Clyde if he was going to host again the following week. He agreed to.

Clyde had a week to prepare. He went to the center staff and reserved a space for the following week. The next day, he went to the pizza restaurant and spoke with the owner, Walli, who agreed to donate a couple of boxes of pizza. Clyde then connected with some of his neighbors who had experience working with youth and asked them to join him at the center. Finally, he borrowed a couple of board games from his friend Louis, who was known for his collection.

A week later, the room was set up, the pizza was ordered, the board games were on the table, and the youth poured in. This happened week after week. The neighborhood adults started to build a rapport with the youth and decided to host a listening conversation. During this conversation, this question was asked: *What is one thing you would like to learn from an adult?* The responses to this question filled sheets of butcher paper that were taped to the walls. Clyde took these sheets, typed them up, and shared copies with the young people the following week. He asked them to vote on the skills they would like to learn. He took the top skills, based on their votes, and brought the results to the connectors. He asked his fellow connectors if they knew any adults who had any of the skills listed. They provided him with several names.

Clyde then contacted those on the list and invited them to join him at the center. Week after week, youth had access to adults who cared and they learned new skills. One week, a youth named Joelle remarked, "I'm learning so much, this is like a library of people," and the name The Skills Library was coined.

One day, as Clyde was setting up the room, a member of the community center staff walked in for a chat. She asked, "How do you know you're making a connection with the youth?" Clyde held out four fingers: "The four-finger test." "What's that?" she asked. Clyde responded, starting with his index finger: "One, you know their name. Two, they know your name. Three, you notice when they are not there. Four, they ask about you when you're not there." He continued, "If you pass this test, you know you've made a connection." This is community. In the words of Rabbi Jonathan Sacks, "A community is where they know your name and where they miss you when you are not there."[2]

7. Gather and Celebrate!

Giftville became known as a place of joy and celebration. Throughout the summer there were block parties that built up to an even bigger event in September, where more than a thousand neighbors got together in the gymnasium of the local high school. As at the community party in late January, they sat around tables of no more than five people. This time their purpose was to share stories of success and what they had learned since their first gathering nearly a year before. After sharing these stories, they shared their vision for the next ten years. Once all neighbors were fully heard and the richness and diversity of possibilities were truly appreciated and celebrated, the neighbors identified which new initiatives they wanted to take forward and commit their efforts and resources to. In effect, they now had a neighborhood plan that was hatched from the inside out.

Through their year of connecting with their neighbors, the folks of Giftville learned to never miss an opportunity to celebrate and give recognition. Regardless of the size of their achievements, all were celebrated, from a cupcake to say thank-you to a neighbor for their thoughtful gesture to an annual Good Neighbors Day celebration where unsung heroes from across the neighborhood were publicly recognized. Celebration shone a bright light on their best and illuminated the joy of community.

8. Assume a Posture, Not a Project

For The Magnificent Seven, the time spent with neighbors in one-on-one conversations was not a project with start and end dates. Rather, it was a posture they wanted to model and introduce into their community's environment. In their approach, what they modeled was listening, connecting, valuing, partnering, and celebrating. Theirs was an attitude that viewed others as gifts to be received rather than as problems to be fixed. It was a posture of abundance, not of scarcity. It was a posture that would outlive them. And that is what a mobilized neighborhood looks like.

Key to the Good Life #8: When it comes to building powerful connections across an entire neighborhood, intentional community building methods are required. Getting beyond traditional community building methods like representative committees, meetings, and debates and moving toward more participatory structures with good dialogue and neighbors searching for common ground requires new approaches. Like trees in a forest need a system of roots in order to flourish, for a culture of care to take root a neighborhood requires some version of an association of associations that reflects its full diversity. Our community power grows as our circles of participation broaden, deepen, and overlap in place..

● ● ●

The story of Giftville started with people, a place, and a newspaper article, then moved to action, with a group of seven people listening to and connecting neighbors. They also engaged with interested associations and scouted for Useful Outsiders. Their actions changed the narrative; years later, outside institutions were talking differently and treating the neighborhood differently. Even the newspaper that previously incited this group had changed its tune; it was now reporting on the potential of Giftville and not on its wounds.

In the end, Giftville is a name of affection for your neighborhood and ours. Imagine what might happen if every neighborhood tried some of the recipes that mobilized the people of Giftville. Imagine a community of joy, connection, and celebration. This might sound like a wild dream, but dreams can come true. Why not? To quote the late civil rights activist and Senator John Lewis,

> "If not us, then who?
> If not now, then when?

CHAPTER 9

The Role of the Useful Outsider

This final chapter looks at ways of shifting neighborhood relationships with outside actors from those of wholesale distrust or unequal power relations to relationships of mutual intent that will result in equitable alliances with what we call Useful Outsiders. Unhelpful Outsiders seek solely to recruit clients to their services and programs, because they view the people in neighborhoods as a bunch of passive consumers. As a result, they inadvertently disable a community's capacity to be active producers. Their view of communities is directly opposite to that of Zita Cobb and Maria Lai.

By contrast, Useful Outsiders seek to be of service to communities, cheering on their alternatives to traditional top-down institutional re-sponses and intentionally featuring community capacities ahead of their institutional capabilities and technologies. They do so because they see neighborhoods as creative and productive places, and they consider that many, if not most, of such community alternatives are likely to have more integrity and local ownership, and to endure for longer.

The neighborhood that has made visible and vital its local resources and functions has the power to teach outsider actors how best to serve them, and the power to defend against outsiders who might harm their neighborhood way of life, whether through good or bad intentions. Rather than expend too much energy on describing the various ways that outside actors can get it wrong or do us harm, we'd like to put the emphasis here on seeking Useful Outsiders to be allies to our cause. Needless to say, harmful outsiders should be spotted quickly and have boundaries placed around them. There are some excellent books that address how best to do that. We especially recommend Jane F. McAlevey's *No Shortcuts: Organizing for Power in the New Gilded Age.*[1]

In the previous two chapters on Mobilizing, we have demonstrated in detail many of the ways in which neighborhoods can mobilize from the inside out. Community building at the neighborhood scale means we can do a lot to produce better outcomes across all seven of the functions discussed in chapter 6. There's a secondary benefit to community building in this way: it prepares the ground for our encounters with outside actors.

Henry Moore and Mick Ward, in their separate roles within city government, were useful outsiders who figured out how to put the resources of their institutions at the disposal of local residents keen to build their communities. Bendigo Bank went one step further and figured out how to organize their many assets to enable neighborhoods in Australia to host and produce their own local banks. Here are their stories and what we have learned from them.

Henry Moore:
Relocating Authority

Henry Moore was the assistant city manager of Savannah, Georgia. In the early 1990s he was responsible for planning and neighborhood development across the city. In this role, he administered millions of dollars of community block grants. After several years of introducing and managing these programs, he decided they had not made much difference in the lives of the people in the neighborhoods—regardless of their intention.

He said that having a leadership position and administering millions of dollars made him feel like he was King Henry. However, measured by outcomes in the lives of local people, he knew he was a failed royal leader.

Therefore, he tried to figure out how he could use his power to produce real change in the neighborhoods he was privileged to serve.

He thought it would be worth seeing whether people in the neighborhoods could produce a better life if he stepped down from his "throne" and gave them some authority. He wrote a letter to each household in the quarter of Savannah where the greatest number of low-income people lived. The letter said that he appreciated what the neighbors had been doing to improve their neighborhood and that he wanted to know what the city of Savannah could do to support their efforts. He said that any local resident could write him a letter (of no more than one page) describing what they would like to do to improve their neighborhood in the coming summer. He then asked that two other people on their block also sign the letter, indicating that they would join in producing the improvement proposed. Finally he said that if the city government could help them achieve their goal, they should let him know. If they needed any money to complete the project, he said he could contribute up to $100 to each idea, although the neighbors couldn't use the money to pay themselves.

About eighty neighbors submitted a proposal, and none of them asked for the entire $100. At the end of the summer, Henry held a dinner celebration at the finest hotel in Savannah for all the neighbors who had been involved in the initiatives. Each block project was presented in a display that could be viewed by all the other participating residents. You could walk through the neighborhoods that had participated and see on every block that there was now a visible leader who had attracted at least two neighbors for mutual gain through joint action.

In the grander scheme of things, over the course of seventeen years, Henry opened up space for and actively sponsored the development of a program to identify and organize resident connectors and promote resident contributions that became visible and valued and encouraged community pride. The program also prompted strong partnerships with community-based organizations, neighborhood residents, local financial institutions, and the housing industry. From 1990 through 1997, these partnerships produced nearly two thousand units of affordable housing and invested more than $50 million to improve inner-city neighborhoods.

Mick Ward:
From Service Provider to Neighborhood Supporter

Between 2013 and 2020, Mick Ward, former deputy director of Health and Care at Leeds City Council in the United Kingdom, took a page from Henry Moore's book. He supported the Neighbourhood Networks across the city of Leeds in order to drive more community-led change, in particular in responding to issues of loneliness and social isolation among seniors. As someone responsible for purchasing services for older people, the choices became ever clearer for him. The first option was to continue to spend on average £40,000 or more purchasing each residential placement, trying to help one older person at a time. He had come to realize that this approach was like pulling people out of the river downstream, often when it was too late to ensure best outcomes and at a point when supports are most costly and life-limiting. The second option was to invest upstream by supporting neighborhood networks engaged in community building across the entire neighborhood in order to come up with local responses that included the gifts of older people. He invited the networks to see older neighbors as needed, not just needy. The networks already had strong asset-based community development impulses and were delighted to explore ways of deepening their impact. Mick and other senior leaders in city government decided year after year to put more energy and resources into the second option, actively cheering on this community effort across Leeds that was creating genuine alternatives to congregated care settings for older people, and doing so close to home, where they were happiest.

Karen Woloszczak, manager at the Gipton Neighborhood Centre in Leeds, recalls how the change of approach and the small investment in asset-based community building had an incredible impact on the outlook of people in the neighborhood. She gives examples of some of the initiatives that have sprung from that change of approach that Mick triggered. Two years ago, a small group of residents wanted to set up a Friday Fish 'n' Chips club. With a no fuss microgrant of £200, she was able to support them in buying the pans and various other bits and pieces they needed to outfit their community kitchen. This completely community-run group now hosts weekly meals where neighbors, young and old, from across Gipton eat together and plot a better community together. As a result, lots of other groups have sprung from this club, including an arts and crafts group, a bingo evening, and a walking group. Karen is their number one cheerleader, but she does not do for them what they can do for themselves. She regularly challenges other professionals to also consider how much more costly traditional services and professionally driven advocacy-based solutions are: "Look how much money you would have to spend sending a staff member to run a coffee morning or day service. This Friday Fish 'n' Chips club is self-sufficient; this initiative is not mine, it's theirs."

Although Mick has retired, the legacy of his work and that of the Neighbourhood Networks and his colleagues continues. The Leeds City Council continues to fund neighborhood-led activities and the employment of community builders across the city. They are very clear that the reason for doing so is to catalyze neighborhoods to mobilize around the seven community functions discussed in chapter 6. One of the City Council's objectives, which is shared by community and voluntary organizations across the city, is for every person in Leeds to have at least three neighbors whom they consider to be their friends. In this way they have successfully reduced the institutionalization of older people by increasing their interdependence at the center of natural and diverse communities.

It's striking to see how Useful Outsiders are popping up in surprising ways around the world. Furthermore, moving beyond individual professionals like Henry and Mick can also be useful. The question becomes whether it is possible for an institution to be a positive precipitator of community action. The growing presence of Bendigo Community Banks in towns and neighborhoods across Australia suggests that it is. They are a powerful example of how even banks can become Useful Outsiders in supporting neighborhood mobilization.

As bigger banks abandoned regional Australia, leaving many communities without branch banking facilities, Bendigo Bank bucked the trend by partnering with local families to enable them to form their own Community Banks. Sparking a community-led movement across the country with the opening of more than 320 Bendigo Community Banks, they have delivered $183 million Australian dollars back into local communities, generating jobs and local economic growth, and a healthy dose of renewed confidence that local assets can be put to good use.

Prospecting for Useful Outsiders

From a community perspective, rather than trying to reform giant institutions like a city government, we are often better off focusing our energies on strengthening our communities from the inside out. That said, we shouldn't stop prospecting for Useful Outsiders like Henry (once his crown slipped) and the supplementary external resources that we consider beneficial (like the microgrants Henry offered with almost no strings attached). Useful Outsiders work in the gap between their institutions and the neighborhoods they serve, just like Mick did. They understand the language and culture of each world and are very realistic about the limits of what they can achieve. They accept the limits of their profession and see treasure in community alternatives. Refreshingly, their actions are not motivated by the drive to harness community assets for the interests of their institution. Instead, they wish to shine a light on the assets and the productivity in the neighborhood and let them be enlisted in a way that benefits local residents.

Over the years, we have witnessed many neighborhoods mobilize toward their preferred future, and quite a few have benefited from the support of Useful Outsiders like Henry and Mick. Both of these public servants looked at neighborhoods through the community lens.

Henry did so by changing his primary question from *How can I use my authority to fix problems and command change?* to *How can I support local residents to come together to make things better where they live?* Henry became a Useful Outsider when he stopped measuring his influence by the quality of his wonderful programs and took a close look at the actual impact of his programs on people's quality of life. The facts were humbling. But through that process he came to understand how to step up in a supportive, nondirective way, and when it was time to step back and cheer the community on.

Aside from the wonderful impacts presented here, the important lesson is that outsiders come in different forms, and they can learn to change.

They can be useful, useless, or harmful. It comes down to how willing they are to see neighbors as doers and neighborhoods as units of production, and their positions and institutional resources as being there to support community-driven change. In short, as Mick says, "It's about relocating authority and using your resources in support of what that relocated and energized authority chooses to do."

Eight Characteristics of a Useful Outsider

In Ireland there is a long tradition of matchmaking, in which a match-maker connects two potential suiters. If you were to ask them how they know the match is a good one, they will say, "Matchmaking isn't something that can be bought or taught. When I meet someone who is a good match for someone else, I know. My instincts guide me." The match between communities and outside actors is often much the same. It is difficult to pin down precisely why some outsiders are useful and some are not, but when you find a Useful Outsider, you know. Thankfully there are some common characteristics of a Useful Outsider. Here are eight:

They serve while stepping backwards. They understand that there are certain things that only communities can do, and that beyond a certain point their professional institutions become useless or potentially harmful. They recognize that in many instances a community response is what is required. Useful Outsiders prefer to be invited into a neighborhood by the people who live there rather than be parachuted in at the whim of an outside institution or expert. They start with the discovery of community capacities. They do not arrive with external "fixes" that other outside helpers have deemed to be what the community needs.

They work to reduce institutional dependency. Useful Outsiders see people primarily as needed, not needy. They work to reduce dependence on outside institutions. They are constantly on the lookout for natural, homespun alternatives to the institutional solution.

They cheer on community alternatives. Useful Outsiders encourage communities to see that they have many invisible capacities that could be productively connected so that they can take on more functions, and they support the community in taking on many of these functions. Here are two examples: (1) a useful doctor will shine a light on a community's health-creating capacities, and (2) a useful law enforcement officer will highlight the safety-producing benefits of neighbors knowing one another by first name and deepening their association with one another outside their homes.

They are open and honest about what they can't or won't do. Useful Outsiders are straight with people. They don't solve problems that do not belong to them, nor do they do things for residents that residents can do themselves or with the support of their neighbors. They operate in the belief that institutions have functions they can usefully perform, but the primary work of community building is in the hands of citizens and must stay there.

They affirm what communities can do. Useful Outsiders lift up the power of community responses. For example, a Useful Outsider will say of loneliness, "You know, there isn't a program or service for loneliness; that's community business." They know that by affirming these community powers they can help others to recognize and value them. They are much like the teacher who connects her pupils with neighborhood elders to learn through oral history about local traditions.

They take an oath: First do no harm. Even before doctors decide what they are going to do to try and help or heal, they promise to first ensure that their interventions do no harm. They do so because they recognize that their efforts in helping can hurt as well as heal. Useful Outsiders in other fields are equally aware of this double-edged sword when it comes to helping. They operate by a similar oath, to do no harm, not just to individuals and their capabilities but also to the associational, cultural, and environmental resources of a neighborhood.

They are interested in reseeding associational life, not just reforming their institutions. Useful Outsiders are motivated by the opportunity to reseed associational life where it is in retreat, and to fan the embers of all associational efforts wherever they are to be found. They have figured out that many of the challenges we face in our lives require the care and power of community—something that their institution cannot produce. Recognizing that most of the things that create a satisfying life are hatched in the nest of community, they have made a decision about where to put their energy. Useful Outsiders act like sidekicks to the neighborhoods they serve, not as slavish servants to their institutions. And so it should be in a democracy. After all, the democratic ideal defines the role of the Useful Outsider as that which happens after the important work that citizens wish to do together has been done.

They are courageous. Useful Outsiders serve two masters, and because they choose to represent community interests, often against the competing interests of their employer, they know that sometimes it's going to cost them. They must be courageous in the face of such challenges. When they advocate for neighborhood interests, they are authentic, assertive, and also compassionate. They prepare well, understand power dynamics, and know how best to surf the waves of red tape and push back against institutional heavy-handedness. Even though they roll with the organizational punches, they remain honest and are often viewed as outsiders (or deviants) by their own institutions. Their colleagues might see them as having "gone native," but for the most part they accept them and their relationships with communities, because they also bring benefits to the institutional world.

Key to the Good Life #9: In forging your way toward the Good Life, remember to preserve community authority to change the things that only you and your neighbors can, and make useful alliances with reliable outsiders who understand how to relocate authority and provide support without directing the outcomes. You will need to audition professionals for the role of Useful Outsider; they are there to be found and they are worth their weight in gold.

• • •

As residents working collectively in our neighborhoods to mobilize toward alternative futures, we should not be afraid to audition outside actors before we invite them into our shared lives. Remember, their job is to support your community, not direct, distrust, or audit it. To paraphrase Lao Tzu, the ancient Chinese philosopher, Useful Outsiders "are best when people barely know they exist. When their work is done, their aim fulfilled, people will say: We did it ourselves."

Three Tools for Mobilization

Tool 1: Mobilizing Community Themed Responses

As one-to-one learning conversations and dialogues at Ideas Fairs mature, themes emerge. Themes are shared concerns or priorities that large numbers of neighbors care about and are willing to work on together. Connectors are excellent at listening for these themes. Once they become apparent, interested neighbors can be convened around such themes to start getting practical about what they understand to be going on in relation to the theme and what might be a good response. It is important to plan such responses with a focus on primary assets (local and within neighborhood influence).

Tool 2: Forming an Association of Associations

An association of associations is a way of building neighborhood power. Just as a choir amplifies individual voices, a group of choirs would amplify and multiply the power of the individual choirs. When we include diversity of associations in the mix, we have a greater array of skills, empathy, creativity, time, and resources. An association of associations is the perfect ground for cultivating a culture of local connections, contributions, coping mechanisms, compassion, and accountability. These elements combine to create a powerful local network that collectivizes local resources in order to maximize what we can generate together and our capacity to hold outside actors to account.

The best way to convene an association of associations is by following the manifest energy of people who care enough to take action like a slow and steady drum beat and by trying the following:

1. **Learning Conversations.** Start by having learning conversations with each of the associations you know locally. Learn about what they do, what they care about, what else they would love to do in the neighborhood. Find out what other associations they have collaborated with. Ask each association you speak with to introduce you to another association that they appreciate and trust. Use this approach to snowball around as many associations as you can.

2. **Community Get-Togethers.** Next, bring together the associations you've had learning conversations with.

3. **Themes.** Share the themes that are emerging in the neighborhood and invite associations to contribute themes that concern them and that they would like to contribute to.

4. **Shared Governance.** Explore ways that associations can organize to promote means of local governance in the neighborhood that include all voices and gifts.

A wide array of new governance structures at neighborhood scale are leading the way. Here is a sample list of experiments currently happening around the world at the neighborhood level. These are just some of the forms of hyper-local democracy that have caught our attention:

- Flatpack Democracy 2.0, https://www.flatpackdemocracy.co.uk/flat pack-democracy-2-0

- Neighbourhood Parliaments, https://neighbourocracy.carrd.co

- Neighborhood plans such as those supported by the Department of Neighborhoods in Seattle, Washington, and by North Ayrshire, Scotland, whose Vibrant Communities team is supporting place-based community plans

- Community benefit societies and cooperatives
- Community land trusts
- Transition Network, https://transitionnetwork.org/about-the-movement /what-is-transition
- Edmonton Federation of Community Leagues, https://efcl.org
- Village In The City, https://villageinthecity.net

Looking across these proven and experimental methods, we can see three different levers being pushed forward. Though the approaches in the preceding list vary widely in approach, all express an interest in community-led production. This is evident in their efforts to support existing local and economic developments. The first lever, then, is to expand the following:

- The number of cooperatives
- Neighborhood-owned, worker-owned, and joint-venture enterprises for producing both exportable and locally useful and intermediate technologies.
- Social financing, community banking, local credit options

These approaches have an explicit agenda to build local productive capacities, which requires new relationships with public sector bodies to ensure increasing relocation of resources and the transfer of real authority to the neighborhood level. The second lever, then, is for an association of associations to use collective power to do the following:

- Undertake forensic analysis of public monies being spent in neighborhoods and devise strategies aimed at shifting their uses away from traditional transfer and maintenance functions and toward investment and animation approaches, such as we are seeing in Milwaukee in the Blueprint for Peace initiative.
- Develop strategies to direct public resources to neighborhood development groups. Local government could return a percentage of neighborhood rates to a local neighborhood treasury. Each household could be allotted a "token," which could be cashed in to provide resources to

a local group. Tracking these tokens would indicate how citizens wish to allocate further resources.

- Work with community foundations to implement models like the Nebraska Community Foundation's Turn Up Your Dream Switch community-building initiative.

The third lever is the commitment to re-root business with the neighborhood economy and sharing economy, thereby actively inserting "locality" into the equation of how businesses make decisions. While economic matters are traditionally a national and international issue, The Bendigo Bank Movement in Australia offers real promise as a model that shows how it can be turned into a local initiative.

Tool 3: Neighborhood Vision

A neighborhood vision or plan that clearly sets out the priorities of the local community, with the backing of all neighborhood associations, connectors, and individual residents, is a powerful vehicle for directing and focusing civic energy toward a preferred future.

There are numerous methods for developing neighborhood plans, and usually a bundle of different ones are used. One of the most popular methods is *Appreciative Inquiry.*

The Appreciative Inquiry process follows four stages, called the 4-D Cycle. The four D's are *Discovery, Dream, Design,* and *Destiny,* in that sequence. Here's what each term means:

- **Discovery:** Residents and their associations, at a community gathering, explore "the best of what is," identifying the neighborhood's strengths, best characteristics, vitality, and where the community is at its best together.

- **Dream:** Residents and their associations imagine a future they really want—a future in which all members of the neighborhood are fully involved in contributing toward that preferred future.

- **Design:** Residents and their associations tap into the best of what is in their neighborhood and in their visions for the future to design high-impact strategies that move the neighborhood creatively and intentionally in their preferred direction.

- **Destiny:** Residents and associations put their strategies into action, making changes as they learn about the impacts of their shared efforts.

The Connected Community—
Not So Wild a Dream!

Benjamin Franklin, in *The Way to Wealth* (1758), wrote:

> For want of a nail the shoe was lost,
> for want of a shoe the horse was lost,
> and for want of a horse the rider was lost,
> being overtaken and slain by the enemy,
> all for want of care
> about a horse-shoe nail.

It's a simple ditty, with a simple but profound message: attend to the small stuff, because it has all kinds of unforeseen yet important impacts on the bigger stuff.

Many of the stories peppered throughout *The Connected Community* are like the biblical tale of David and Goliath, in which the little guy triumphs against the odds. Such stories remind us that bigger is not necessarily better and doesn't always win the day. The local stories we've shared here, in the face of so many significant global challenges, encourage neighbors to work together to make "small" the new "big." Because if we don't, we may find that it is not just our local economies that become displaced, but also our health and well-being, safety, environment, and democracy itself.

To paraphrase Benjamin Franklin:

> For want of a neighbor the neighborhood was lost,
> for want of a neighborhood the citizen was lost,
> and for want of a citizen democracy was lost,
> being overtaken by the Giants of industry, technology,
>   and globalization,
> all for want of care
> about a neighbor.

Each time we go out of our way to encourage, support, share, and enjoy a neighbor, we are putting the world to rights on our own street. What better way is there to finish our conversation than to reaffirm the neighborly principles that have been featured throughout this book. These principles can act as our true north in transforming the invisible neighborhood into a visible, vivid, and vibrant neighborhood on our journey toward the Connected Community.

We have commended six neighborly principles (which are also practices or acts) above all others:

1. **Discover** one another and what surrounds you.
2. **Welcome** one another and the stranger.
3. **Portray** one another and your neighborhood in terms of your gifts.
4. **Share** what you have to secure what your neighborhood wants.
5. **Celebrate** one another's comings and goings, the plantings and harvests.
6. **Envision** with one another towards a preferred future.

Each act opens the way toward a culture of care in the Connected Community. Around the world, lovers of community do the following:

Discover. Lovers of community discover other local resident connectors who naturally weave together their community through neighbor-to-neighbor and associational relationship-building. They convene tables of connectors whose membership overlaps and represents the diversity of an entire neighborhood.

Welcome. They actively welcome neighbors—and those who are pushed to the margins—through inclusive learning conversations and listening campaigns. Learning conversations and listening campaigns surface what people care about enough act to on with their neighbors.

Portray. As people discover what they care about enough to take collective action on, creating dynamic portraits of the local assets they can use is a helpful way of making community building blocks visible to everyone. No one person can hold a full picture of all the ingredients that a neighborhood encompasses. Therefore, creating a shared portrait of your neighborhood assets is a powerful way of enabling your neighbors to discover what community-building ingredients they all already have. Then they can figure out how best to connect these unconnected resources in ways that create new possibilities and resolve old problems.

Share. Intentionally doing things together, from breaking bread to tending a neighborhood garden, brings us into a radical presence with our neighbors. Sometimes it is necessary to create "shareable moments." These moments occur when we intentionally create the conditions for neighbors to have exchanges. Such shareable moments can include skills exchanges, seed swaps, books, toys, and repair cafes, where residents bring broken items to be fixed and small electrical items to be repaired. They create a community on-ramp for people who may be unsure about how to get into community life. The more these moments enable gift exchange (the giving and receiving of gifts), hospitality and association, the more likely they will become part of a community's customs and traditions.

Celebrate. Celebrating neighborliness and community life through local rituals, annual events, parties, sports events, yard sales, and front porch concerts are important ways to give ourselves a collective slap on the back. Adding food, fun, songs, and dance into the mix is a great way to honor our past achievements and dream up new community possibilities.

Envision. Creating a collective vision that establishes the priorities and reveals the possibilities for the shared future of a neighborhood is a powerful way of binding the community together. It ensures that residents in the neighborhood own the vision.

Here is the last story we'd like to share with you. We feel it brings all the threads of our journey through this book into the tapestry we have woven together.

A Story from Wisconsin, USA: Jazz and the Structure of Powerful Communities

During the first year of the COVID-19 pandemic, many neighborhood organizations and block clubs stopped their traditional face-to-face meetings. Nonetheless, in many locations these groups spontaneously initiated innovative community activities. In many neighborhoods with no community groups, new and unprecedented initiatives were begun.

One example of these local innovations is a neighborhood of eight hundred households in the older industrial city of Menasha, Wisconsin. A report on the pandemic responses in that neighborhood indicated that the following creative activities occurred:

- Forty residents responded to a telephone invitation to provide help to neighbors when needed.
- An outdoor "jump-around" party on one block evolved into a physically distanced but socially connected parade on many blocks; residents were joined by neighbor-owned classic cars.
- Two hundred loaves of bread contributed by a food pantry were distributed to neighbors.
- Neighbors who were "essential workers" were recognized by tying blue ribbons around trees bordering the street.
- Two "mansion-size" outdoor food pantry houses were built and stocked by neighbors.
- Six local businesses agreed to sell fundraising candy bars, with the proceeds going to help keep the food pantries stocked.
- The annual Boy Scout food drive was cancelled, so local Boy Scout families organized a neighborhood food drive that collected contributions from nearly one hundred local residents.

- On New Year's Eve there was an outdoor party in the local park for all residents. It included bell ringing and neighbors making resolutions for the year ahead.

One active neighborhood member noted that all of these activities occurred without any face-to-face formal meetings and with only one collective Zoom gathering.

Meetings are one method for making citizen decisions at the neighborhood level, but in this and many other places there have been very few or no meetings, in person or virtually, since the onset of COVID-19. However, as the Menasha report indicates, many decisions were made that resulted in many forms of citizen mobilization and action. If there were very few meetings of any kind, how can we explain the process by which the decisions were made that preceded these countless local initiatives?

Perhaps an analogy can be useful here. Consider a jazz club in a big city. It's 2:00 A.M. and in most clubs the jazz musicians' work is done. However, some musicians want to keep on playing, so they go to a club that is licensed to be open after 2:00 A.M.—an "after hours" club. Three or four jazz musicians gather at the club and set up their equipment at the front of the room. Some players know some of the others while some don't know any of the others.

Suddenly they begin to play a wonderful jazz piece. They have no written music and most of them don't know the other players. How can this happen? They are creating music that is so free, innovative, and open-ended—yet perfectly coherent. The musicians play together and play individually, with no apparent structure or order. In this they are like the neighbors in Menasha, Wisconsin.

The innovation and improvisation that happens in jazz occurs because there is an invisible structure encompassing the players. The structure has three elements: a melody, a key, and a rhythm. That's why, before they begin, one musician says, "How about 'Don't Get Around Much Anymore' in B-flat?" The others nod and the drummer sets the time. The three-part structure is now manifest, and improvisation can take place within it.

This musical process is an analogous structure that can help us understand how the invisible innovative decision-making occurred in Menasha without decision-making meetings or apparent traditional leadership. A way to understand the Connected Community structure is to focus on the context where the dispersed decision-making occurs: the *connectorship*. It is a context that creates a structure that enables innovative citizenship to emerge.

The context has three elements:

1. **Communality.** The residents in the area have a common affinity. Regardless of other resident differences or disagreements, these place-based common affinities can grow from the desire to enjoy, celebrate, entertain, and so on. The affinity can be a crisis such as the pandemic. It can be a possibility—we want to create a park. It may be a fear, such as the threat of gentrification. It can be the love of the place—our place, remembered in stories that inspire and capture successful neighborhood activities of the past.

2. **Individual Capacities.** Every neighbor believes that they have some special and significant gift, talent, skill, or knowledge. This belief is often the core of their sense of self-worth. It is this self-worthiness that residents are willing and often waiting to contribute on behalf of their own particular community. These capacities are the basic community-building tools.

3. **Connectivity.** The local capacities of most neighbors are latent. There must be some precipitate that brings them to life. That precipitate is connectivity. Through the connection of neighbors' capacities, power is created, citizenship emerges, and democracy is lived.

The invisible structure of productive communities where decision-making and leadership are dispersed comes from a neighborhood with unique commonalities, unique capacities, and common connectivity. In these kinds of places, where citizen creativity is visible, what is not usually present in any traditional form is a central leader or formal decision-making. Nonetheless, a focus on the structure needed for citizen productivity can provide an appropriate framework for understanding the beautiful civic music being played in the Menasha neighborhood and in millions more like it. They are creating "leaderful" and "decisionful" democracies.

* * *

One reason that community-driven movements have spread worldwide is because they are based on revealing the community structure that provides the "nest" from which health, wealth, and power is born and grows. In this book, it has been our great joy and privilege to share local knowledge, experience, and stories that make visible the three C's of community: *commonality, capacity,* and *connectivity.*

As strange as it may sound, we cannot truly commit to our neighborhoods until we become disenchanted by them. Neighborhoods are not enchanted places; they have baggage and history and are filled with fallibility and limitations. But like the late, great Canadian singer-songwriter Leonard Cohen reminds us, "There is a crack, a crack in everything / that's how the light gets in." There are limits to local solutions; there are issues that require global responses. Still, although local actions are not sufficient to address all of life's challenges, they remain essential to all our futures. It is through fallibility that possibility is revealed, and through possibility that creativity and productivity emerges. In this book, we have, we hope, revealed some of the possibilities and creativity that lie in wait in the places we call our neighborhoods. Our neighborhoods hold, in their modesty, huge potential for a healthy, prosperous, and powerful life for all and our planet.

The Connected Community offers a vision that is handmade and homespun, woven by the gifts of every person, association, and local place. It does not place the sole hope for our futures in the hands of our leaders. Instead it says, "Come on, join us; we need you. We can make a difference, we can be one another's hope; together we will rise. And you know, it's not so wild a dream; the raw materials surround you. Now go, make the invisible visible. We'll meet you on the sacred ground that now is the visible neighborhood, the Connected Community. Save us a seat on the park bench. We'll feed the birds and cherish our children together."

The Connected Community at a Glance

	The Disconnected Neighborhood	The Connected Community	Keys to the Good Life
	Definition: Prioritizes relationships outside the neighborhood that separate neighbors from one another and promotes individual survival over community wellbeing."	**Definition:** Nurtures neighborhood relationships that enable people to work together to create a Good Life.	**Definition:** Key lessons learned from neighborhoods on their journey toward deeper connection.
	Chapter 1 is about shifting our mindset.		
DISCOVER	*Disconnected* **Mindset:** Often overlooks local resources; takes the bait of the consumer story: Your Good Life is in the marketplace (externally focused).	*Connected* **Mindset:** Looks first to what you/we already have before seeking a market solution. Doesn't overlook local solutions (internally focused).	**Key #1:** The extent to which we personally flourish is tied to how much our neighbors and our neighborhoods are flourishing. Hence our Good Life is found in our communities and local economies, not in distant marketplaces.

The Disconnected Neighborhood	The Connected Community	Keys to the Good Life
Chapter 2 is about shifting from a deficit- to an asset-based map.		
Disconnected **Map:** Portrays the neighborhood as a glass half empty, with too many problems and deficits for local people to start creating a decent life together.	*Connected* **Map:** Portrays the neighborhood as a glass half full, with enough assets to begin to create a decent life for everyone in the neighborhood.	**Key #2:** Refuse to allow others to use maps of misery to define you. Define your course of Discovery by starting with what's strong and you'll get to what wrong in better shape to face life's inevitable challenges.
Chapter 3 is about (where possible) locally sourcing the ingredients we use for our well-being in place of costly remote assets.		
Disconnected **Ingredients:** 1. Contributions of individuals outside the neighborhood. 2. Remote institutions. 3. Physical assets outside the neighborhood. 4. External economic exchanges. 5. Consumer culture.	*Connected* **Ingredients:** 1. Contributions of residents. 2. Associations. 3. Local institutions. 4. Neighborhoods' built and natural environments. 5. Local economies, not financial exchanges. 6. Stories and local heritage.	**Key #3:** The Good Life is found "between" us and our neighbors, us and our ecology, us and our economy, us and our culture. The Good Life is like a good cake: before you can make it you've got to find the ingredients.

DISCOVER

	The Disconnected Neighborhood	The Connected Community	Keys to the Good Life
CONNECT	Chapter 4 is about shifting away from overreliance on leaders and toward connectors and connectorship.		
	Disconnected **Responsibility:** The challenge is to get external leaders to get their act together, and to find residents with leadership capacity and provide them with the necessary training to improve their personal influence and impact. Leaders are the answer.	*Connected* **Responsibility:** The challenge is to broaden circles of participation and ensure that associational life deepens. Connectors are essential to this challenge and to welcoming strangers at the edge. This challenge is about connectorship.	**Key #4:** The great innovations in life are mostly not the result of very clever people inventing new and extraordinary things. More often than not they are the result of regular, savvy people connecting ordinary things in extraordinary ways.
	Chapter 5 is about shifting away from viewing our neighbors as apathetic and toward seeing them as eager to contribute if asked.		
	Disconnected **Attitude:** Our neighbors are too selfish, too busy, too stressed, too distracted, and too apathetic to care about their neighbors/ neighborhood.	*Connected* **Attitude:** Our neighbors and their associations are more active than any one person can know, and many who are not yet active are waiting to be invited to contribute to the common good.	**Key #5:** One of the best-kept secrets of modern life is that our neighbors are happy to contribute and receive gifts, but there's a catch: they are waiting to be asked. So, the Good Life cannot be achieved without an element of positive risk.

	The Disconnected Neighborhood	The Connected Community	Keys to the Good Life
	Chapter 6 is about shifting away from seeing our neighborhoods as units of consumption to seeing them as units of production.		
CONNECT	*Disconnected* **Purpose:** Our shared purpose as neighbors is to individually consume our common wealth by purchasing or by advocating that institutions assume essential functions in the areas of health, safety, raising our children, economic and ecological stewardship, care, and production of food that appeals to diverse personal preferences, regardless of environmental impact.	*Connected* **Purpose:** Our shared purpose as neighbors is to produce the common good by assuming essential functions in the areas of health, safety, raising our children, economic and ecological stewardship, care, and local carbon-neutral production of nutritious food.	**Key #6:** The purpose of a neighborhood is to create a context and the essentials for a Good Life to be had by all who live there. For that purpose to come into everyday reality, neighbors have to take on some functions that only neighbors and their associations can perform. It is through such collective actions that we discover our community powers.
	Chapter 7 is about the practical methods we can use to mobilize community power from crisis to connections.		
MOBILIZE	*Disconnected* **Methods:** Leaders, planning, deficit/needs mapping, advocating for reform.	*Connected* **Methods:** Circle of connectors, learning conversations, asset mapping.	**Key #7:** Don't wait for a flood; instead, initiate a listening campaign in your neighborhood; give your neighbors a good listening to.

	The Disconnected Neighborhood	The Connected Community	Keys to the Good Life
MOBILIZE	Chapter 8 is about the practical methods we can use to mobilize community power from envisioning to collective action.		
	Disconnected **Methods:** Leaders, planning, deficit/needs mapping, advocating for reform.	*Connected* **Methods:** Community building, dialogue, parties/celebrations/hosting.	Key #8: The Good Life is made up of individual and associational gifts that are like shards of different-colored glass that form a mosaic. That mosaic is the context in which our personal stories and those of our neighbors and place combine.
	Chapter 9 is about shifting neighborhood relationships with outside actors away from wholesale distrust or unhealthy dependence and toward points of mutual intent that will result in useful alliances with Useful Outsiders.		
	Disconnected **Orientation:** Seeks to recruit clients to their services/programs. Views neighborhoods as units of consumption.	*Connected* **Orientation:** Seeks to be useful to community life; cheers on community alternatives and features community capacities. Sees neighborhoods as creative and productive places.	Key #9: Preserve community authority to change the things that only you and your neighbors can change, and make useful alliances with reliable outsiders who understand how to relocate authority and provide support without directing the outcomes.

The Connected Community
Discussion Guide

We hope that reading *The Connected Community* has provided you with tools and inspiration as you discover, connect, and mobilize the gifts in your neighborhood.

The discussion prompts in this guide are intended simply to provide support as you and your neighbors gain your footing. We encourage you to move at a pace that best suits your own community-building efforts. Take the time you need, and savor the moments spent with others. This guide is a compass, not a map. It will help you to navigate the basic argument of the book and, in itself, is another tool to assist you in making the invisible visible in your neighborhood, thereby precipitating community-building initiatives that make local assets visible, connected, and vibrant.

Here are some tips for hosting a discussion:

- Find a place where participants can be close to one another.
- Sit in a circle, not behind tables.
- If the group is large, break into smaller groups of three, then come back and share reflections and insights with the larger group.
- Have food and drinks present. Food is a connector of people.
- Move through the questions at your own pace.

- Sixty- to ninety-minute sessions are ideal.
- Devote a portion of the time to storytelling.
- Add your own questions to those included here.

Discover

1. Homecoming: Rediscovering the Value of Community

"One of the hidden dangers of consumer culture is that it sometimes baits us into overlooking local assets in favor of specialized external services or goods. And though local assets are not sufficient on their own to respond to all of life's challenges, they are essential to a decent, satisfying, and inclusive life."

- What are some ways you have overlooked local assets?
- What is something you have done for yourself that would typically have been done for you?
- Do you have a story that comes out of this experience?
- What gifts did you recognize in yourself and in others?
- Looking beyond this experience, what gifts are present in your community that people tend not to see?

2. The Hazards of the Wrong Map

Chapter 2 notes that neighborhoods are regularly portrayed in one of two ways:

1. Most frequently, the neighborhood is portrayed as a glass half empty, with too many problems and deficits for local people to start creating a decent life together.

2. The neighborhood is portrayed as a glass half full, with enough assets to begin to create a decent life for everyone in the neighborhood. In this picture, local people are also confident that they have the power to leverage in additional or supplementary assets from outside when needed.

- How has your neighborhood been portrayed?
- Who or what has helped to shape this perspective?
- How does this perspective make you feel about yourself?
- How does this perspective make you feel about your neighborhood?

3. The Neighborhood Treasure Hunt

After everyone has responded to the following question, decide as a group on that "thing" you would like to address. With the six essential ingredients in mind, identify the local resources that would help you move forward on the identified issue.

- What is something you are concerned about and care enough about to act on?

Contributions of Residents

- What is something you are good at?
- What do you know well enough to teach?
- What would you like to learn?
- What ways would you like to get involved in your neighborhood?
- What is your hope for your neighborhood?

Based on what was shared, what are the gifts, skills, passions, and knowledge that can be used in your collective effort?

1. _____   2. _____

3. _____   4. _____

5. _____   6. _____

7. _____   8. _____

9. _____   10. _____

Associations

- What associations do you belong to?
- What associations are you aware of?
- What do these associations do that help people other than the members of their association?
- What are they willing to do that they are currently not doing?

Of the clubs, groups, and networks of unpaid citizens you know of or are connected to, which ones would be of use to your initiative?

1. _____   2. _____

3. _____   4. _____

5. _____   6. _____

7. _____   8. _____

9. _____   10. _____

Local Institutions

- What are some local institutions that you know of or are connected to?
- How are these local institutions currently serving the community?
- What are ways they have supported community initiatives?
- In what ways have they been community-serving?

Of the local institutions mentioned, whether for-profit, nonprofit, nongovernmental or governmental organizations, which ones align with what you are trying to do?

1. _____   2. _____

3. _____   4. _____

5. _____   6. _____

7. _____   8. _____

9. _____   10. _____

Local Places

- Where are the places that people gather?
- What spaces are available for community initiatives?
- Where do people like to meet?

The main stage on which these three human resources of a given neighborhood—(1) the individual, (2) the associational, and (3) the institutional—are revealed, connected, and brought into productive collective action is the built and natural environment. What small, local, bounded places are available to you that can be a resource for community building?

1. _____ 2. _____

3. _____ 4. _____

5. _____ 6. _____

7. _____ 8. _____

9. _____ 10. _____

Exchange

- Where are the places that people give freely of their time to one another?
- Where are the places where people can freely swap items?
- What businesses/institutions tend to hire local individuals?
- What businesses/institutions support and participate in local initiatives?

Of the places and businesses/institutions discussed, list those that best fit with what you are looking to do in your neighborhood:

1. _____ 2. _____

3. _____ 4. _____

5. _____ 6. _____

7. _____ 8. _____

9. _____ 10. _____

Local Stories

- Do you remember a time when members of this community worked together?
- Was there a time when you felt connected to others in your community?
- What makes you proud of your community?
- Do you have stories about times you included people who are often excluded in other neighborhoods?

Local culture, or "the community way," often finds expression within stories of people and the "ways" in which they have learned through time to survive and thrive within their home places. Stories further enable us to pass on important life lessons and traditions to the further generations. What are some lessons learned from the stories shared?

1. _____

2. _____

3. _____

4. _____

5. _____

Connect

4. Beyond Leaders toward Connectors

"Knowing just six neighbors significantly enhances the mental health of each person and reduces the impacts of life's stressors, including significant events like the coronavirus pandemic."

- With how many neighbors are you on first name terms?
- How did you come to connect with them?
- Have any of these neighbors connected you to other neighbors?
- Do any of the people mentioned exhibit any of the six main connector characteristics?

- Are they part of your discussion group while reading this book? If not, how would you go about inviting them?

5. The Community Is Waiting to Contribute

"In every neighborhood there is a powerful unused potential for creative work, problem-solving, and the creation of a culture of contribution."

- Where do you feel the unused potential is in your neighborhood?
- Share stories of times when you have experienced acts of neighborliness/generosity in your neighborhood.
- In pairs, share those things you would be willing to share for free with a neighbor, and those things you would like to receive from a neighbor (such as gardening tips, recipes, care for a pet while you're away).
- Reconvene as a larger group. Share the things you would like to offer and receive. How do these offerings connect to the issue you wanted to address in the discussion of chapter 3?
- What are some practical ways you can support neighbors beyond your group to share their offers, wants, and experiences with one another?

6. The Seven Functions of Connected Communities

"Each neighborhood is like a loom: the seven functions are the threads, and the interconnections between these functions create a tapestry that reveals the health, wealth, and power of the Connected Community."

- Review the seven functions listed in chapter 6
  In what way(s) do you believe they are already being performed
  in your neighborhood?
- Share a story of how one or more of the functions have been active
  in your life.

- In your story, who was involved in fulfilling the function(s)? Are they part of your group? How would you include those neighbors who are not currently invited?

- Explore how those who were involved in fulfilling a function could buddy up. For example, how can those with a passion for homegrown produce link with those who care deeply about health and well-being?

Mobilize

7. Step by Step from Crisis to Connected

"They were searching for answers, possibilities, and connections, not a plan. In the end, they were guided by their instincts, their trust in one another, and their commitment to their neighborhood."

- What in the story of Giftsville has inspired you?
- How is your neighborhood similar or dissimilar to Giftsville?
- What are some of the things they did that you can potentially add to your initiatives?
- What would you have done differently than folks in Giftville?

8. Step by Step from Envisioning to Collective Action

As a group, using chapter 8 as a guide, put a community-building process on paper. Here are some questions to consider:

- What themes are you trying to address?
- Who are the connectors in your neighborhood?
- What questions would you like to ask in your learning conversations (neighborhood listening campaign)?
- What resources do you have access to (such as meeting space, funds, and so on)?
- How will you communicate your effort to the broader neighborhood?
- Who isn't currently involved in this effort that should be?

- What is the timeframe for this initiative? Are you traveling at a pace that allows trust to be built—in other words, going at the local pace or at the pace of someone outside the community?

- As you proceed with your process, regularly review your progress and document the lessons you are learning along the way.

9. The Role of the Useful Outsider

"Useful Outsiders seek to be of service to communities, cheering on their community alternatives to traditional top-down institutional responses, and intentionally featuring community capacities ahead of their institutional capabilities and technologies. They do so because they see neighborhoods as creative and productive places."

- Who do you consider to be the Useful Outsiders in your neighborhood?

- How would you describe your current relationship with them?

- Describe the relationship you would like to have with them?

- How could they potentially assist in your initiative?

- What are some of the boundaries you need to put in place when inviting/working with Useful Outsiders?

Conclusion: The Connected Community—Not So Wild a Dream!

You have come to the end of the book, but the journey doesn't end. Take time in this session to celebrate. Maybe listen to some jazz, share some food, and discuss what these sessions have meant to you. Here are some questions you can ask:

- Because of these discussions, what is now present or visible in your life that wasn't present or visible before?

- What is something good you have recognized in yourself and others?

- Who in the group has shared a gift with you? Name them and tell the story.

- In what ways has your neighborhood become more connected because you chose to gather around this book?

Sharing Your Connected Community Story

Cormac and John would love to hear about your adventures in building the Connected Community in your neighborhood. Please share your neighborhood stories on this dedicated online platform and enjoy the stories of other Connected Communities from neighborhoods around the world: https://theconnected.community/

Notes and Sources

Foreword

1. Whitman, Walt. 2015. *Leaves of Grass.* Canterbury Classics.

Introduction

1. Carothers, Thomas. 2019. "How to Understand the Global Spread of Political Polarization." Carnegie Endowment for International Peace. https://carnegieen dowment.org/2019/10/01/how-to-understand-global-spread-of-political -polarization-pub-79893.
2. Kretzmann, John P., and John McKnight. 1993. *Building Communities from the Inside Out: A Path Toward Finding and Mobilizing a Community's Assets.* Asset-Based Community Development Institute, Institute for Policy Research, North-western University.
3. Putnam, Robert. 2000. *Bowling Alone.* Simon & Schuster.
4. Holt-Lunstad, Julianne, Timothy B. Smith, Mark Baker, Tyler Harris, and David Stephenson. 2015. "Loneliness and Social Isolation as Risk Factors for Mortality: A Meta-Analytic Review." *Perspectives on Psychological Science* 10 (2): 227–37. https://doi.org/10.1177/1745691614568352.
5. Eisenstein, Charles. 2018. *Climate: A New Story.* North Atlantic Books. Eisenstein argues that "a story of separateness" has dominated how we think about ourselves, one another, and our planet. The antidote, he proposes, is a replacement (better) story that curates a more interdependent set of connections—what he terms "interspecies" relatedness.

Chapter One

1. E. F. Schumacher popularized this term in his best-selling book *Small Is Beautiful*, 1973.
2. Sampson, Robert. 2013. "When Disaster Strikes, It's Survival of the Sociable." New Scientist 2916: 28–29. https://scholar.harvard.edu/sampson/publications /when-disaster-strikes-its-survival-sociable.

Chapter Four

1. "Take the #KINDChallenge." Nextdoor. 2020. http://go.nextdoor.com/kind -challenge-us.

Chapter Six

1. Holt-Lunstad, Julianne, Timothy B. Smith, and Jay Bradley Layton. 2010. "Social Relationships and Mortality Risk: A Meta-Analytic Review." https://journals. plos.org/plosmedicine/article?id=10.1371/journal.pmed.1000316. In this controlled study carried out over a 7.5-year period, social relationships are found to be more effective than any other risk factor in helping individuals, matched for disease status, age, and excluding suicide and pet relationships, to live long, well lives. Particularly telling is the way the results dwarf the impact of hypertension treatment. Additional research on the impacts of loneliness can be found at https://pubmed.ncbi.nlm.nih.gov/25910392 and Holt-Lunstad's evidence submitted to the American Academy of Sciences can be found at https://www.national academies.org/our-work/the-health-and-medical-dimensions-of-social-isolation -and-loneliness-in-older-adults.
2. Putnam, *Bowling Alone,* pp. 327–331.
3. Sampson, "When Disaster Strikes, It's Survival of the Sociable."
4. "Blueprint for Peace." n.d. https://city.milwaukee.gov/414Life/Blueprint.
5. "Soul of the Community." 2010. Knight Foundation. https://knightfoundation .org/sotc.

Chapter Eight

1. Block, Peter. 2009. *Community: The Structure of Belonging.* Berrett-Koehler.
2. Sacks, Jonathan. 2013. *To Heal a Fractured World: The Ethics of Responsibility.* Bloomsbury Academic, p. 54.

Chapter Nine

1. McAlevey, Jane. F. 2018. *No Shortcuts: Organizing for Power in the New Gilded Age.* Oxford University Press.

The We Can Game

The We Can Game is an ABCD tool developed by Cormac Russell of the ABCD Institute and is directly based on the Capacity Inventory developed by John P. Kretzmann and John McKnight for *Building Communities from the Inside Out: A Path Toward Finding and Mobilizing a Community's Assets* (Institute for Policy Research, 1993, pp. 19–25). The game has been developed in direct consultation with John P. Kretzmann and John McKnight.

The purpose of this game is fourfold:

1. It is a fun way for a group's members to learn about one another.

2. It provides an actual experience of what a Capacity Inventory is, and why it is useful.

3. It provides an early portrait of community capacities and of key connectors who are not yet in the room who can connect and bring these capacities in the direction of productive action.

4. It creates an ideal framework for discussing ABCD.

Facilitator's Guide

This guide has been developed as a support to facilitators. The following suggested steps were developed after playing the original game with several hundred groups around the world. However, that does not mean you can't play the game in another way that makes sense to you. In fact, we encourage you to find new and creative ways to develop and enjoy this game.

- The facilitator invites the larger group to form small groups of about ten. Each group of ten forms a circle, preferably sitting down either on the floor or in a chair.
- In the middle of the circle, place four Sorting Cards. The Sorting Cards should be used to form the corners of a square.
- Lay out the four cards as follows:

  #1 We Can.

  #2 We Know Who Can.

  #3 We Can't and We Don't Know Who Can.

  #4 Who Else/What Else?

- As you lay out the cards, explain out loud what you are doing: "I'm setting out the game. These are the categories we're going to use to think about community capacities. They will help us to identify what community capacities we have close at hand."
- Scatter the 100 Capacity Cards on the floor between the Sorting Cards; ask people to scan them.
- Using a log sheet, ask each person in the group to guess what percentage (how many) of the 100 Capacity Cards will go into the *We Can* pile. If it helps, you can give people a printout of the following list of capacities in large print. This can be done in different accessible forms so that people can play the game from their seat with support.
- The log sheet will be a simple page with space for each group member's name and their individual guesses. A facilitator can create this on flip chart paper. Once everyone has made a guess, post the log sheet where everyone can see it.

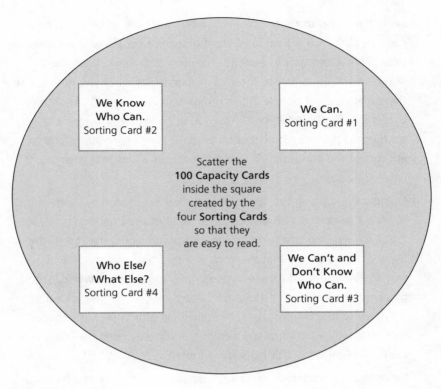

Sample Log Sheet

Name	Guess % We Can

- Invite the group to choose two volunteers who will act as connection spotters. Their job will be to notice if groups of people with similar talents/capacities start to emerge. They will note their observations at the end of the exercise. Their job will be to say, "Did you notice that there were a lot of people in this group who are gifted at DIY, music, gardening, food production?" Your job as facilitator is to create space for them at the end of the session to make such observations and to encourage the group to talk about the opportunities that emerge, when they do.

- Going around the group, ask whoever is willing to read out some cards to take a random bunch of cards. The facilitator will need to be clear that each member of the group has a responsibility to the rest of the participants to ensure that everyone is supported to participate in a way that feels right for them. For example, some people will want to play from their seat by reading the Capacity list (as mentioned earlier; they may have difficulty seeing the cards any other way); others may wish to listen as the cards are read out. Some may need the cards in braille, and others in picture/graphic format.

- Going counterclockwise, invite each person who has taken a bunch of Capacity Cards to each in turn read one card and then ask the group which category of Sorting Card they should place the Capacity Cards around. Here the sequence matters. As each card is read, the facilitator will ask, "Can anyone in our group do this?" If you don't get a response, try noting that people do not have to be able to do it to a professional standard.

- If after offering this reassurance, still nobody in the group responds with "I can," go on to ask, "Do we know anyone locally who can and would do it if we asked them?" Another way of asking the question is, "Do you know anyone who can do this and who's good for a favor?"

- As participants identify people they know, encourage them to name the person, place their name on one of the blank cards, and put the name in the *Who Else/What Else* category/sorting pile. When people are placing the Category Cards down, they should place them around the appropriate Sorting Card in a circle so that everyone can see exactly what, for example, the group can do.

Here's an example:

> **Reader:** Baking.
>
> **Facilitator:** Can anyone do this? Please indicate if you can do this.
>
> **Participant #1:** I can bake. I make a mean Vienna roll.
>
> **Participant #2:** I can, but I haven't done it in years. I used to do it when my husband was alive.
>
> **Facilitator:** That's wonderful. Thank you. Is there anybody else who can bake in the group?

The facilitator then prompts the participant who read the card to place the card around the *We Can* Sorting Card.

If no one in the group can bake, the facilitator will go on to say, "OK, that's fine, we can't. Do we know anyone who can?" If no, place the card in the third category, *We can't and we don't know who can.*

- Once all the Capacity Cards have been read out and placed down, ask three volunteers to count the Capacity Cards around each of the Sorting Cards, one volunteer per Sorting Card.
- Compare the number of cards in the *We Can* category to the guesses recorded on the log. Facilitate a discussion around the differences. Typically there will be a pretty big difference.
- Now take out some Blank Cards and ask people what other gifts people feel they'd like to share to help build up their community. Place in the *Who Else/What Else* category.
- Now ask participants to name other people they know who can make contributions. Again, place the names on the Blank Cards and around the Sorting Card *Who Else/What Else.*
- Then ask if there are any agencies or individual professionals who make important contributions to helping people come together to do things that matter to them.

- Now ask where the encounter spaces are, the places where people regularly meet to exchange their capacities at the local level. Offer some typical examples: farmers' market, outside the school, and so on.
- Ask each participant to list the clubs, groups, and formal and informal networks they are part of.
- Group process discussion: turn to the connection spotters and invite them to comment on any connections they may have noticed.
- Lead a general discussion around the question, *What could we do with all of this to build a stronger community?*

Capacity Inventory

The Capacity Cards are directly based on the work of the ABCD Institute and specifically seek to use *The Capacity Inventory* developed by John P. Kretzmann and John McKnight. Following is an abridged version that lists the capacities we have focused on. Reprinted and amended with permission of John P. Kretzmann and John McKnight, from *Building Communities from the Inside Out: A Path Toward Finding and Mobilizing a Community's Assets* (Institute for Policy Research, 1993, pp. 19–25).

Capacity Inventory (Skills Information)

Health

1. Care for Older People
2. Care for the Emotionally Distressed
3. Care for the Sick
4. Care for People with Disabilities
5. Helping First-Time Mothers
6. Breast Feeding Support
7. Preparing Special Diets
8. Exercising
9. Fashion Advice
10. Visiting a Neighbor
11. Putting People at Their Ease

Office

12. Knowledge of Social Media
13. Paperwork for Small Businesses
14. Taking Inquiries for Charities
15. Taking Inquiries for Small Businesses
16. Setting up a Database
17. Keeping Track of Supplies
18. Bookkeeping
19. Computer Skills

Construction and Repair

20. Painting a Room
21. General House Repairs
22. Knocking Out Walls
23. Wall Papering
24. Furniture Repairs
25. Repairing Locks
26. Building Sheds
27. Bathroom/Kitchen Modernization
28. Installing Insulation
29. Plumbing Repairs
30. Electrical Repairs
31. Bricklaying and Masonry
32. Furniture Making
33. Plastering
34. Soldering and Welding
35. Heating System Installation
36. Installing Windows
37. Carpentry Skills
38. Roofing Repair

Maintenance

39. Window Washing
40. Floor Waxing or Mopping

41. Washing and Cleaning Carpets/Rugs
42. General Household Cleaning
43. Fixing Leaky Taps/Faucets
44. Mowing Lawns
45. Plants and Caring for Gardens
46. Pruning Trees and Shrubbery
47. Wood Stripping/Refinishing

Food

48. Catering
49. Serving Food to Large Numbers
50. Preparing Meals for Large Numbers
51. Clearing/Setting Tables for Large Numbers
52. Operating Commercial Food Preparation Equipment
53. Bartending
54. Baking

Child Care

55. Caring for Young Children
56. Caring for Older Children
57. Caring for Teenagers

Transportation

58. Driving a Car
59. Driving a Van
60. Driving a Bus
61. Driving a Tractor Trailer
62. Driving a Commercial Truck/Lorry
63. Driving a Vehicle/Delivering Goods

Operating Equipment and Repairing Machinery

64. Repairing Radios, TVs, and so on
65. Repairing Other Small Appliances

66. Car Repairs
67. Repairing Trucks/Buses
68. Using a Forklift
69. Repairing Large Household Equipment (such as refrigerator)
70. Fixing Washers/Dryers

Supervision

71. Writing Reports
72. Filling Out Forms
73. Planning Projects
74. Making a Budget
75. Keeping Records of All Your Activities
76. Interviewing People

Sales

77. Handling Cash Transactions
78. Selling Products Wholesale
79. Selling Products Retail
80. Selling Services
81. Door-to-Door selling
82. Music
83. Singing
84. Playing an Instrument
85. Starting a Band
86. Manage a Band
87. Teaching an Instrument

Other

88. Knitting and Other Needlecraft
89. House Removals
90. Managing Property
91. Assisting in the Classroom
92. Hairdresser

Community Skills

93. Leading a Boy Scouts/Girl Scouts Group
94. Organizing a Fundraiser
95. Running a Bingo Session
96. Volunteering for School-Parent Associations
97. Coaching a Sports Team
98. Organizing Field Trips
99. Organizing a Street Party
100. Starting a Community Garden
101. Outreach in Community for Inclusion

The game can be found at: https://theconnected.community/images /theconnectedcommunity/site/contents/The-We-Can-Game.pdf

Chapter 5 Tables

Gifts of Seventeen Residents of Three Blocks in Chicago's Woodlawn Neighborhood	
Solution-driven	Good with kids
Motivator	Problem-solving
People person	Connecting with others
Organized	Objectivity
Ability to plan, strategize, and implement change	Hardworking
	Articulate
Creative	Multitasker
Managerial	Voiceovers (radio)
Education	Commentating
Business	Public speaking
Veteran services	Bringing diverse groups together
Leader	Interacting well with youth
Political analyst	Intense motivator
Getting things done	Ability to inspire people
Vision	Dealing with kids well
Ability to create	Encourager
Good listener	Reading comprehension
Cooking	Good with people
Mentor	Computers
Good communicator	Mathematics
Discernment	Reaching out
Good with hands	

Skills of Seventeen Residents of Three Blocks in Chicago's Woodlawn Neighborhood	
Computer troubleshooting	Home improvement
Gourmet cooking	Human development and mobilization
Artist	
Writing	Psychology
Blogging	Negotiation
Mentoring young women	Entrepreneur
Sewing	Legal knowledge (occupation attorney)
Singing	
Teaching	Business
Strategic-planning skills	Painting
Reading	Cooking
Business (financial)	Master gardener
Identifying strengths	Grant writing
Caretaker	Financial aid assistance (students)
Cooking	Interior decorator
Medical assistant	Project manager
Carpentry	Knitting
Electrical work	Light repairs
Plumbing	Computers
Sheet metal worker by profession	Mathematics
Gardening	Researching
Landscaping	Skating
Decorating	Real estate law
Community organizing	People problem-solving
Handyman	Computer skills
	Housekeeping

Passions of Seventeen Residents of Three Blocks in Chicago's Woodlawn Neighborhood

Educational justice for youth

Business strategy (for local and small businesses to move community forward)

Educating people

Politics

Community development

Facilitating youth activities

Spirituality

Global socioeconomics

Motivational

Problem solver

Service to others

Occupational work

Horticulture (gardening)

The outdoors

Advocating for an environmentally friendly community

Bike riding

Youth

Community Organizing events (celebratory)

Music

Youth involved in music

Directing cultural events

Mentoring young women

Family (i.e., children)

Business development

Community outreach

Youth initiatives

Senior initiatives

Job training

Personal financing

Working out

Reading

Sincere Milk Ministries (i.e., military moms)

Helping in general

Education

Skating

Correcting problem buildings

Church

Listening to jazz

Literacy

Etiquette

Decorating

Handwork

Wall hangings

Secondhand store shopping

Good eye for potential

Dressing

Antique shopping

Gardening

Photography

Working with kids

Being around people

Being able to help someone

Teachables of Seventeen Residents of Three Blocks in Chicago's Woodlawn Neighborhood

Entrepreneurship	Home schooling
Job creation	Basic etiquette
Job training	Breastfeeding techniques for first-time moms
Marketing	
Strategic planning	First aid
Physical fitness	Hygiene
Basic accounting	Self-esteem
Economics	Life skills for youth
How to review a credit report	Knitting
Credit quality	Computer technology
Banking	Mathematics
Dietician	Skating
Organizing events	How to be a good neighbor
English	Real estate
Public speaking	Reading comprehension
Presentational etiquette	Sewing
Cooking	Handcrafting
Journalism for beginners	Cooking
	Grammar

Acknowledgments

A book like this is produced by a community and not simply by two authors whose names happen to appear on the cover. We are simply the note-takers in this endeavor. First and foremost, we want to express our deep appreciation and admiration for all those whose stories give substance and authenticity to this book. Your generosity and commitment to everyone around you continues to prove the power of Connected Communities in word and deed. We also wish to acknowledge those countless stories that lack of space prevented us from sharing. We carry your example in our hearts; you are our North Star as we seek out the hidden treasures that surround us.

To all those who helped us crowdsource the title of this book, we thank you and hope that you are as proud of the title and the contents as we are.

Special thanks go to our friend and fellow traveler Parker Palmer, who kindly wrote the foreword to this book. Parker is a much-loved elder and way finder in the movement toward more community-centered ways of being in the world. We have learned more from him than we can ever hope to share.

We owe a huge debt of gratitude to Tom Dewar, Colleen Quinn, Howard Lawrence, Sandy Dyson Reid, Thomas Hayes, Angela Fell, Jonathan Massimi, Peter Robinson, Judah Armani, Julian Abel, and Simon Duffy, all of whom worked tirelessly to review the many early versions of the book's manuscript. Your comments, suggested enhancements, and encouragement were invaluable and have made the book into a more readable and enjoyable offering than we as authors could have ever hoped to achieve on our own.

We are especially grateful to Joop Hofman, Beth Mount, David Hasbury, Jackie Reid, Scott Jones, and Olivia Butterworth, whose commitment to welcoming the stranger at the edge of neighborhoods is legendary. Their vigilance in constantly lifting up the question, "How are we welcoming the gifts of the stranger?" has helped us to sharpen our thinking about how best to build the Connected Community from the edges in.

Finally, we wish to acknowledge the support of our families, friends and, neighbors, without whom we could not have written this book.

Index

A

ABCD (Asset-Based Community Development) approach, x, xiv, 3, 38

ABCD (Asset-Based Community Development) Institute, 3, 7, 177, 182

abundance mindset, 7

The Abundant Community, 64

Appreciative Inquiry, 148–49

assets (building blocks)
  definition of, 3
  dynamic portraits of, 153
  interdependence of, 51
  list of, 41, 44–50
  mapping, 55–56
  treasure hunt for, 41–43, 55–56
  universal nature of, 3, 51

associations
  association of, 46, 63, 145–48
  average number belonged to, 78
  characteristics of, 44–45
  contributions of, 45–46, 78, 80–82
  definition of, 44
  inventory of, 126
  local governance and, 146
  names of, 80
  uncovering, 112–13, 126–27
  Useful Outsiders and, 142–43

B

The Bendigo Bank Movement, 136, 139–40, 148

Block, Peter, 64

Blueprint for Peace, 91, 147

Bowling Alone, 5

Brixton Pound, 49

building blocks. *See* assets

Building Communities from the Inside Out (The Green Book), x, 3, 177, 182

C

Cahn, Edgar, 49

capacities, individual, 156, 157

Capacity Inventory, 177, 182–86

care, co-creating, 95–97
celebrating, 131, 153
change
    nature of, 2–3
    neighborhoods as units of, 4
Chicago, 75, 76, 97–98, 187–90
children, raising, 94–95
Clarke, Jenny, 65–67
climate change, 23–24, 92
Coalville, England, 35–39, 74
Cobb, Alan and Tony, 25
Cobb, Zita, 6, 24–28, 74, 135
Cohen, Leonard, 157
communality, 156, 157
community. *See also* Connected
        Community
    definition of, 2
    three C's of, 156, 157
community authority, 107, 143
community get-togethers, 120–24,
        131, 146
community walk, 55–56, 125
conflicts, resolving, 127–28
Connected Community
    asset-based map of, 18
    attitude of, 58
    building blocks of, 41–51
    definition of, 2, 18, 58, 70, 106
    as foundation, 2–4
    framework for creating, 110
    functions of, 85–86, 88–99
    Good Life and, 2
    imagining, 5
    ingredients for well-being in, 19
    journey toward, 10–14
    mindset of, 18
    mobilization methods in, 106
    neighborly principles of, 152–54
    orientation of, 107
    responsibility in, 58, 61
    shared purpose in, 59
    structure of, 156

Connecting stage
    components of, 57
    at a glance, 58–59
    tools for, 101–4
connections
    creating, 119–20
    types of, 62–63
    value of, 62
connectivity, 156, 157
connectors
    circle of, 69
    examples of, 64–67
    finding, 64, 101–2, 111–12,
        116–18
    hallmarks of, 63, 101
    importance of, 61
    leadership and, 69
    main characteristics of, 67–68
    power of, 63–64
connectorship
    definition of, 69–70
    tribalism vs., 70
    value of, 70–71, 156
conscience, gifts of the, 54, 114
consumerism, 21, 25
Cooper, Chelsey, 32, 34
COVID-19 pandemic, 33, 62, 66,
        154–55, 156
Cox, John, 95
culture, 50
curiosity, importance of, 116
currencies
    alternative, 49
    fiat, 49

D
Dads on Duty, 95
development
    capacity-focused, 3
    traditional deficit-based approach to,
        3–4, 35
Deventer, Netherlands, 8–10

disconnected neighborhood
  attitude of, 58
  deficit-based map of, 18
  definition of, 18, 58, 106
  ingredients for well-being in,
    19
  mindset of, 18
  mobilization methods in, 106
  orientation of, 107
  responsibility in, 58, 61
  shared purpose in, 59
disconnection, effects of, ix–x, 1.
  See also loneliness
Discover-Explore-Connect questions,
  115
Discovery stage
  commitment to, 26
  components of, 17
  at a glance, 18–19
  tools for, 53–56
discussion guide, 165–73

E
Eastcott, Don, 90
ecology, stewarding, 91–92
economies, local, 6, 28, 92–93
Edinburgh, Scotland, 65–67
Edmonton, Alberta, 64–65, 67, 69,
  76, 89–91, 147
Eigg, 23–24, 28, 92
energy, 91–92
exchange, 48–50
experience, definition of, 44

F
Flatpack Democracy 2.0, 146
Fletcher, Gordon, 95–96
Fogo Island, 6, 24–28, 74
food production, 93–94
Fortier, Catherine, 95
4-D Cycle, 148–49
Franklin, Benjamin, 151, 152

G
Gallup, 93
gifts
  categorizing, 113–15
  definition of, 44
  discovering, 113, 118
  exchanging, 75–78, 83
  Gifts of the Head, Heart, Hands,
    and Conscience exercise, 53–54
Gipton Neighborhood Centre, 138
Go Ahead Eagles, 9
Good Life
  Connected Community and, 2
  keys to, 14, 18–19, 28–29, 38, 50–51,
    58–59, 70, 83, 99, 106–7, 118, 132,
    143
  Ubuntu and, xiii–xiv
governance, shared, 146–48
governments, role of, 14–15
The Green Book. *See Building Communities from the Inside Out*

H
Hancock, Paul, 66
hands, gifts of the, 54, 114
happiness, source of, 50–51
head, gifts of the, 53, 114
health
  connections and, 62
  enabling, 89–90
  loneliness and, 5–6
Heaney, Seamus, 32
heart, gifts of the, 53–54, 114
Highlands, 64–65

I
Ideas Fairs, 103–4, 124–25, 145
individualism, xiv
institutions, local, 46–47
intangibles, exchange of, 48
I Wish You Enough movement,
  93–94

K

Kenyon, Peter, 69
Kibera, 45, 73
Knight Foundation, 93
knowledge
    definition of, 44
    sharing, 75–78
Kretzmann, John P., x, 3, 177, 182

L

Lai, Maria, 6, 86–87, 99, 135
Lao Tzu, 144
Lawrence, Howard, 64–65
leadership, limits of, 69
learning conversations, 102–3, 146
Leeds, 138–39
Lewis, C. S., 25
Lewis, John, 133
listening campaigns, 102–3, 111, 118
localism, 21–24, 29
loneliness
    effects of, ix–x, 5–6
    prevalence of, 5
Lunstad, Julianne Holt, 89

M

maps, deficit- vs. asset-based, 18, 31–39
McAlevey, Jane F., 136
McKergow, Mark, 65–67
Melbourne, Australia, 32
Menasha, Wisconsin, 154–56
Milwaukee, Minnesota, 91
mindset, shifting, 7
Mobilization stage
    components of, 105
    at a glance, 106–7
    tools for, 145–49
Montrose, Australia, 32–35, 38, 39
Montrose Giving Tree, 33, 74
Moore, Henry, 136–37, 140

N

Nairobi, Kenya, 45, 73
Nebraska Community Foundation, 148
needs assessment, 35
neighborhoods. *See also* Connected Community; disconnected neighborhood
    building blocks of, 41–51
    definition of, 2
    economies of, 6, 28, 92–93
    health and, 5–6
    outward appearance vs. reality of, 73–74
    power and, 7–8
    purpose of, 59, 85, 99
    two approaches to portraying, 31–32
    as units of change, 4
    unused potential in, 81, 157
    wealth and, 6–7
neighborhood vision/plan
    developing, 148–49
    power of, 148, 153–54
neighborly principles, 152–54
Neighbourhood Networks, 138–39
Neighbourhood Parliaments, 146
North Ayrshire, Scotland, 146
North Glenora, 89–91
No Shortcuts, 136

O

outsiders, 127, 135–36. *See also* Unhelpful Outsiders; Useful Outsiders

P

Park, Peter, 95
passions
    definition of, 44
    sharing, 75–78
    peace-building practices, 127–28
People First movement, x, 96–97
places, local, 47–48

power, source of, 7–8
"protest versus progress" debate, 1–2
Putnam, Robert, 5–6

R
residents, contributions of, 44
Ruston, Richard, 95

S
Sacks, Rabbi Jonathan, 131
safety, 90–91
Sampson, Robert, 24
Savannah, Georgia, 136–37
scarcity mindset, 7
Seattle, Washington, 146
security, ensuring, 90–91
Self Advocacy Development Project, 96
shareable moments, 153
sharing economy, 49–50
Shorefast Foundation, 25–27
Shreveport, Louisiana, 95
Sinatra, Frank, xiv
Singapore, 93–94
skills
    definition of, 44
    library, 129–31
    sharing, 75–78
The Soul of Community, 93
Southwood High School, 95
Spring Green, Wisconsin, 78–82
stories, local, 50, 116–17
Street Gardens Academy, 9

T
tangibles, exchange of, 48
Tassajara Cooking, 109
tenacity, importance of, 117–18

themes, 145, 146
TimeBanking, 49
Toronto, Ontario, 96
Transition Network, 147
tribalism, 70
Turn Up Your Dream Switch, 148
Tutu, Bishop Desmond, xiii

U
Ubuntu, xiii–xiv, xv
Ulassai, Sardinia, 6, 86–88
Unhelpful Outsiders, 14, 135
Useful Outsiders
    characteristics of, 141–43, 144
    examples of, 136–40
    prospecting for, 132, 136, 140–41, 144
    Unhelpful Outsiders vs., 135

V
Vibrant Communities, 146
Village In The City (VITC) initiative, 65–67, 69, 147
Voorstad neighborhood, 8–10

W
Ward, Mick, 136, 138–39, 140, 141
wealth, 6–7, 28, 92–93
The We Can Game, 54–55, 177–86
welcoming, 153
Whitman, Walt, xi–xii
Woloszczak, Karen, 138–39
Woodlawn, 76–78, 187–90
Worth, Pat, x–xi, 95–97

Y
Young, Paul, 95
"youth problem," 95, 129

About the Authors

John McKnight (left) and Cormac Russell (right)

Cormac Russell

For more than thirty years, Cormac has been fascinated by how people and places weave together to find common purpose. Like a three-legged stool, the themes of people, place, and purpose have grounded and defined his life and work. He was raised in County Limerick, in the west of Ireland, in the village of Patrickswell.

In the early 1990s, Cormac began working with the Irish Health Board, as it was known at that time. Professionally trained in therapeutic approaches and psychological models, he worked with children and young people who were wards of court, attempting to support them into community care settings in neighborhoods, as far away from formal institutions as possible. It was here that he learned the limits of institutional interventions, especially well-intended ones. It became painfully clear to him that taking young people who had experienced profound disruption and trauma and placing them in a new house in a strange neighborhood with others who had similar stories was not a genuine expression of "community care."

This work triggered a question that haunted him for many years and still drives him to this day: How many others are at the edge of our communities, living in our neighborhoods, but apart from us in every other sense? This question has come to define Cormac and his work. It was on the back of this question that he discovered John McKnight. Cormac and John's connection blossomed into a deep friendship and working collaboration that has spanned more than two decades.

In 1996, Cormac established Nurture Development, a social enterprise dedicated to discovering meaningful ways to build communities from the inside out, with a real welcome for the stranger at the edge. Since then, his work has contributed to the emergence of more community-centered approaches in four continents. In 2015, he published *Asset-Based Community Development: Looking Back to Look Forward,* which provides an insight into the intellectual heritage of ABCD and traces the people who had the most influence on John McKnight's thinking.

In 2020, Cormac published his second book, *Rekindling Democracy: A Professional's Guide to Working in Citizen Space,* in which he sets out his vision for deeper local democracy and argues that the way to get there is to realize that neighborhoods are the most important unit of change.

It in this book that he addresses the third leg of the stool: purpose. Writing *The Connected Community* with John has enabled Cormac to bring the three legs of the stool even closer together. His curiosity about people has settled on the question of the Connected Community. His focus on place has landed on neighborhoods, and his interest in purpose has become about restoring a culture of community.

Cormac lives with his wife, Colleen, and their children and neighbors in South County Dublin. You can visit his website at nurturedevelopment. org and communityrenewal.learnworlds.com

John McKnight

John was raised a traveling Ohioan, living in seven neighborhoods and small towns in the eighteen years before he left to attend Northwestern University in Evanston, Illinois. There he had the good fortune to be educated by a faculty dedicated to preparing students for effective citizenship. He graduated into the U.S. Navy, where he had three years of "postgraduate" education in Asia during the Korean War.

John returned to Chicago and began working for several activist organizations, including the Chicago Commission for Human Relations, the first municipal civil rights agency. There he learned the Saul Alinsky trade called *community organizing*. This experience was followed by the directorship of the Illinois American Civil Liberties Union, where he organized local chapters throughout the state.

When John Kennedy was elected president, John was recruited into the federal government, where he worked with a new agency that created the affirmative action program. Later he was appointed Midwest director of the United States Commission on Civil Rights, where he worked with local civil rights and neighborhood organizations.

In 1969, John's alma mater, Northwestern University, invited him to return and help initiate a new department called the Center for Urban Affairs, a group of interdisciplinary faculty doing research designed to support urban change agents and progressive urban policy. John's appointment was an act of heroism on the part of the university, because it gave him a tenured professorship though he had only a bachelor's degree.

While at the center and at its successor, the Institute for Policy Research, John and a few of his colleagues focused their research on urban neighborhoods. The best-known result of this work was the formulation of an understanding of neighborhoods focused on the usefulness of local resources, capacities, and relationships. This work was documented in a guide titled *Building Communities from the Inside Out,* which describes an approach to community building that became a major development strategy practiced in North and South America, Europe, Africa, Asia, and Australia. As an aside, it was during this time that he was one of the trainers of Barack Obama as he learned the skills of community organizing.

John is also the author of *The Careless Society,* a classic critique of professionalized social services and a celebration of communities' ability to heal themselves from within. He lives with his wife in Evanston, Illinois. You can visit his website at www.abcdinstitute.org

About
Nurture Development,
the Community Renewal Centre,
and the ABCD Institute

About Nurture Development

Nurture Development is a training, research, and development consultancy founded by Cormac Russell in 1996. Today it has a global portfolio, working extensively in 36 countries to influence how institutions (for-profit and not-for-profit; governmental and nongovernmental) serve communities and work in citizen space.

For further information visit www.nurturedevelopment.org
or email info@nurturedevelopment.org

About the Community Renewal Centre (CRC)

The Community Renewal Centre is the online arm of Nurture Development, established to extend its reach and impact. The CRC delivers online training and real-time mentoring supports to organizations that want to strategically and practically embed Asset-Based Community Development (ABCD) and other strengths-based approaches in the way they work. Organizations can be at one or more points of entry to more community-centered ways of working and the CRC can tailor its supports to match your current reality. The Centre works internationally with senior policymakers and political and executive leaders to embed community-centered frameworks into policing, health, criminal justice, social care, and economic and environmental policy. We also support organizations with service transformation and whole-systems change. The aim of the CRC is to provide world-class training and consultancy for all professions working in citizen space, from frontline practitioners to politicians at the local, state, and federal levels of government.

For further information visit https://communityrenewal.learnworlds.com. To explore support and collaboration, email Colleen Quinn at colleen@nurturedevelopment.org

About the ABCD Institute

The Asset-Based Community Development Institute is at the center of a large and growing movement that considers local assets as the primary building blocks of sustainable community development. Building on the skills of local residents, the power of local associations, and the supportive functions of local institutions, ABCD draws upon existing community strengths to build stronger, more sustainable communities for the future.

We invite you to learn about the Institute and its work in the university and community context. We hope you will join us in building strong communities. The ABCD Institute is partnered with and housed at DePaul University's Irwin W. Steans Center for Community-Based Service Learning & Community Service Studies in Chicago, Illinois.

Berrett–Koehler
Publishers

Berrett-Koehler is an independent publisher dedicated to an ambitious mission: *Connecting people and ideas to create a world that works for all.*

Our publications span many formats, including print, digital, audio, and video. We also offer online resources, training, and gatherings. And we will continue expanding our products and services to advance our mission.

We believe that the solutions to the world's problems will come from all of us, working at all levels: in our society, in our organizations, and in our own lives. Our publications and resources offer pathways to creating a more just, equitable, and sustainable society. They help people make their organizations more humane, democratic, diverse, and effective (and we don't think there's any contradiction there). And they guide people in creating positive change in their own lives and aligning their personal practices with their aspirations for a better world.

And we strive to practice what we preach through what we call "The BK Way." At the core of this approach is *stewardship,* a deep sense of responsibility to administer the company for the benefit of all of our stakeholder groups, including authors, customers, employees, investors, service providers, sales partners, and the communities and environment around us. Everything we do is built around stewardship and our other core values of *quality, partnership, inclusion,* and *sustainability.*

This is why Berrett-Koehler is the first book publishing company to be both a B Corporation (a rigorous certification) and a benefit corporation (a for-profit legal status), which together require us to adhere to the highest standards for corporate, social, and environmental performance. And it is why we have instituted many pioneering practices (which you can learn about at www.bkconnection.com), including the Berrett-Koehler Constitution, the Bill of Rights and Responsibilities for BK Authors, and our unique Author Days.

We are grateful to our readers, authors, and other friends who are supporting our mission. We ask you to share with us examples of how BK publications and resources are making a difference in your lives, organizations, and communities at www.bkconnection.com/impact.

Dear reader,

Thank you for picking up this book and welcome to the worldwide BK community! You're joining a special group of people who have come together to create positive change in their lives, organizations, and communities.

What's BK all about?

Our mission is to connect people and ideas to create a world that works for all.

Why? Our communities, organizations, and lives get bogged down by old paradigms of self-interest, exclusion, hierarchy, and privilege. But we believe that can change. That's why we seek the leading experts on these challenges—and share their actionable ideas with you.

A welcome gift

To help you get started, we'd like to offer you a **free copy** of one of our bestselling ebooks:

www.bkconnection.com/welcome

When you claim your **free ebook**, you'll also be subscribed to our blog.

Our freshest insights

Access the best new tools and ideas for leaders at all levels on our blog at ideas.bkconnection.com.

Sincerely,

Your friends at Berrett-Koehler

Certified

B

Corporation